PROGRAMS IN BASIC FOR ELECTRONIC ENGINEERS, TECHNICIANS & EXPERIMENTERS

Other TAB books by the author:

No. 771 *Integrated Circuits Guidebook*
No. 861 *Display Electronics*
No. 960 *IC Function Locator*
No. 1000 *57 Practical Programs & Games in BASIC*
No. 1055 *The BASIC Cookbook*
No. 1085 *24 Tested, Ready-To-Run Programs in BASIC*

PROGRAMS IN BASIC FOR ELECTRONIC ENGINEERS, TECHNICIANS & EXPERIMENTERS

by Ken Tracton

FIRST EDITION

FIRST PRINTING—JANUARY 1979
SECOND PRINTING—DECEMBER 1979
THIRD PRINTING—APRIL 1981

Printed in the United States of America

Library of Congress Cataloging in Publication Data

Tracton, Ken.
Programs in BASIC for electronic engineers, technicians & experimenters.

Includes index.
1. Electronics—Data processing. 2. Electronics—Computer programs. 3. BASIC (Computer program language) I. Title.
TK7835.T7 621.381'025'5425 78-21928
ISBN 0-8306-9858-2
ISBN 0-8306-1095-2 pbk.

Cover photo courtesy of Texas Instruments.

Preface

As the BASIC language is becoming the favorite of the micro-users and small-computer people, more-advanced programs are required to take full advantage of the machines. This book contains a mix of programs to satisfy the needs of as many users as practical.

All the programs have been fully tested, and most of the actual listings provided as original manuscript. Plotting is an essential requirement in many fields of endeavor and in different disciplines. To be able to see a result graphically can make a world of difference to the user.

I extend my thanks to Mr. T., who knows what I mean.

Ken Tracton

Dedication

Dedicated to all the little computers in the world, and may they grow up some day.

Contents

AC VOLTAGES

The AC Voltage program will convert among peak, effective, and average of sinusoidal waveforms. You can convert from any one to another. Three entries are required: First enter "convert from," then "convert to," and finally the "value of the first."

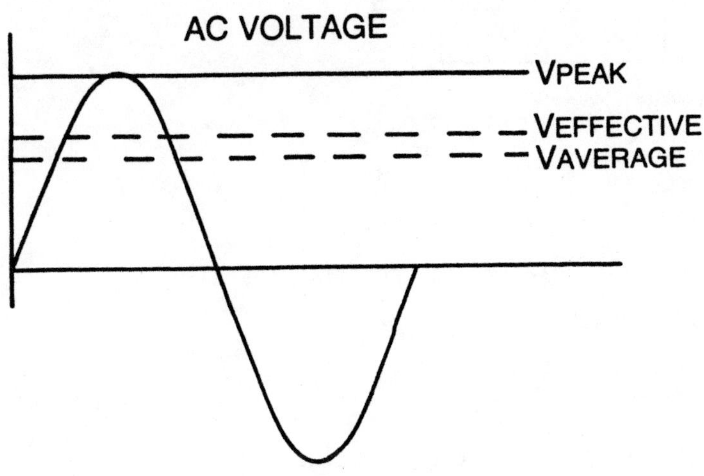

VPEAK = 1.414 VEFFECTIVE

VAVERAGE = 0.637 VPEAK

VAVERAGE = 0.9 VEFFECTIVE

AC Voltage

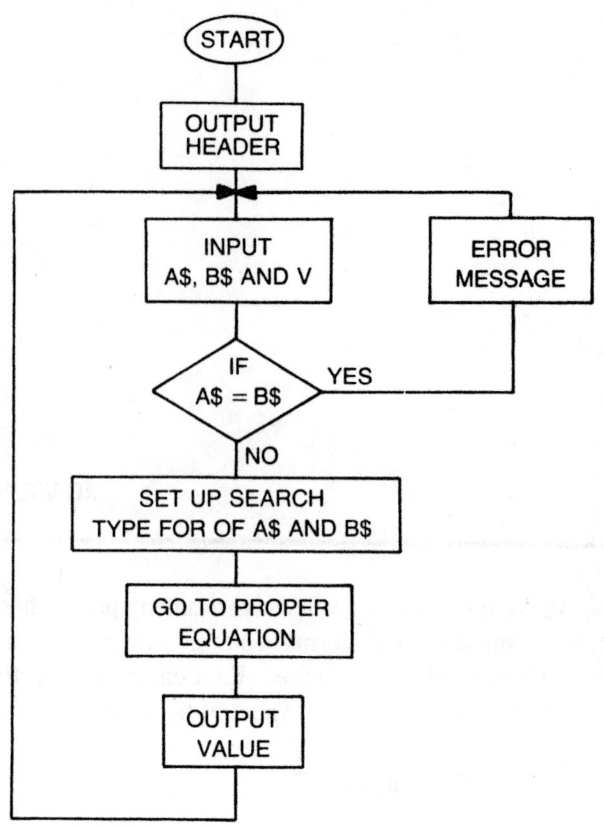

AC Voltage

```
EXAMPLE

RUN

ENTER P FOR PEAK, E FOR EFFECTIVE AND

A FOR AVERAGE

INPUT FORMAT IS AS FOLLOWS;

X,Y,Z

WHERE THE FIRST TWO X'S ARE EITHER

P,E OR A, AND THE Z IS THE VALUE OF

THE 1ST X, WE ARE CONVERTING FROM 1ST

TO 2ND MEASUREMENT.
```

```
ENTER

?E,A,20

AVERAGE VOLTAGE IS 18 VOLTS

ENTER

? STOP

RUN COMPLETE
```

AC VOLTAGES

```
00010  REM THIS PROGRAM CONVERTS
       BETWEEN DIFFERENT
00020  REM MEASUREMENTS OF AC VOLTAGES
00030  REM KT 1978
00040  PRINT
00050  PRINT ''ENTER P FOR PEAK, E FOR
       EFFECTIVE''
00060  PRINT ''AND A FOR AVERAGE''
00070  PRINT ''INPUT FORMAT IS AS
       FOLLOWS;''
00080  PRINT ''X,X,Z''
00090  PRINT ''WHERE THE FIRST TWO X'S
       ARE EITHER''
00100  PRINT ''P,E OR A, AND THE Z IS
       THE VALUE OF''
00110  PRINT ''THE 1ST X. WE ARE CON-
       VERTING FROM 1ST''
00120  PRINT ''TO 2ND MEASUREMENT''
00130  PRINT
00140  PRINT ''ENTER''
00150  INPUT A$, B$,V
00160  IF A$ = B$ THEN 180
00170  GOTO 700
```

```
00180  PRINT ''THE FIRST TWO ENTRIES
       MUST BE DIFFERENT''
00190  GOTO 140
00200  IF A$ = ''P'' THEN 260
00210  IF A$ = ''E'' THEN 290
00220  IF A$ = ''A'' THEN 320
00230  PRINT ''THE ENTRIES MUST BE
       EITHER A,P OR E''
00240  PRINT
00250  GOTO 140
00260  IF B$ = ''E'' THEN 350
00270  IF B$ = ''A'' THEN 400
00280  GOTO 230
00290  IF B$ = ''P'' THEN 450
00300  IF B$ = ''A'' THEN 500
00310  GOTO 230
00320  IF B$ = ''P'' THEN 550
00330  IF B$ = ''E'' THEN 600
00340  GOTO 230
00350  REM CONVERT FROM P TO E
00360  X = V/1.414
00370  PRINT
00380  PRINT ''THE EFFECTIVE VOLTAGE
       IS '';X; ''VOLTS''
00390  GOTO 130
00400  REM CONVERT FROM P TO A
00410  X = 0.637*V
00420  PRINT
00430  PRINT ''AVERAGE VOLTAGE IS '';
       X; ''VOLTS''
```

```
00440  GOTO 130
00450  REM CONVERT FROM E TO P
00460  X = 1.414*V
00470  PRINT ''PEAK''
00480  PRINT ''THE PEAK VOLTAGE IS
       '';X; ''VOLTS''
00490  GOTO 130
00500  REM CONVERT FROM E TO A
00510  X = 0.9*V
00520  PRINT ''PEAK''
00530  PRINT ''THE AVERAGE VOLTAGE IS
       '';X; ''VOLTS''
00540  GOTO 130
00550  REM CONVERT FROM A TO P
00560  X = V/0.637
00570  PRINT
00580  PRINT ''THE PEAK VOLTAGE IS
       '';X; ''VOLTS''
00590  GOTO 130
00600  REM CONVERT FROM A TO E
00610  X = V/0.9
00620  PRINT
00630  PRINT ''EFFECTIVE VOLTAGE IS
       '';V; ''VOLTS''
00640  GOTO 130
```

BASE CONVERSION

Base Conversion will allow the user to convert any base 10 (decimal) number to any base from 2 to 16, which includes binary, octal and hexadecimal. This is very useful with computers having front panels which must be programmed by binary, octal or hex keys.

```
EXAMPLE

THIS PROGRAM ACCEPTS A POSITIVE INTEGER
IN BASE 10 (RADIX 10), AND WILL CONVERT IT
TO ANY BASE FROM 2 TO 16

----------------------------------------
DESIRED BASE IS ? 2

INTEGER (RADIX 10) =  ? 1949
----------------------------------------

 1949  RADIX 10 =  1  1  1  1  0  0  1  1  1  0  1  BASE  2

----------------------------------------
DESIRED BASE IS ? 3

INTEGER (RADIX 10) =  ? 3328
----------------------------------------

 3328  RADIX 10 =  1  1  1  2  0  0  2  1  BASE  3

----------------------------------------
```

```
DESIRED BASE IS ? 4

INTEGER (RADIX 10) =  ? 123421
----------------------------------------

 123421  RADIX 10 =  1  3  2  0  2  0  1  3  1  BASE  4


----------------------------------------
DESIRED BASE IS ? 5

INTEGER (RADIX 10) =  ? 123
----------------------------------------

 123  RADIX 10 =  4  4  3  BASE  5


----------------------------------------
DESIRED BASE IS ? 6

INTEGER (RADIX 10) =  ? 7865
----------------------------------------

 7865  RADIX 10 =  1  0  0  2  2  5  BASE  6


----------------------------------------
DESIRED BASE IS ? 7

INTEGER (RADIX 10) =  ? 5678

----------------------------------------


 5678  RADIX 10 =  2  2  3  6  1  BASE  7


----------------------------------------
DESIRED BASE IS ? 8

INTEGER (RADIX 10) =  ? 4326
----------------------------------------

 4326  RADIX 10 =  1  0  3  4  6  BASE  8


----------------------------------------
DESIRED BASE IS ? 9

INTEGER (RADIX 10) =  ? 34901
----------------------------------------

 34901  RADIX 10 =  5  2  7  7  8  BASE


----------------------------------------
DESIRED BASE IS ? 10

INTEGER (RADIX 10) =  ? 1978
----------------------------------------
```

```
 1978  RADIX 10 =  1  9  7  8  BASE  10

----------------------------------------
DESIRED BASE IS ? 11

INTEGER (RADIX 10) =  ? 1234
----------------------------------------

 1234  RADIX 10 = A 2  2  BASE  11

----------------------------------------
DESIRED BASE IS ? 12

INTEGER (RADIX 10) =  ? 341278
----------------------------------------

 341278  RADIX 10 =  1  4  5  5 BA BASE  12

----------------------------------------
DESIRED BASE IS ? 13

INTEGER (RADIX 10) =  ? 3478
----------------------------------------

 3478  RADIX 10 =  1  7  7  7  BASE  13

----------------------------------------
DESIRED BASE IS ? 14

INTEGER (RADIX 10) =  ? 23908
----------------------------------------

 23908  RADIX 10 =  8  9 DA BASE  14

----------------------------------------
DESIRED BASE IS ? 15

INTEGER (RADIX 10) =  ? 23657
----------------------------------------

 23657  RADIX 10 =  7  0  2  2  BASE  15

----------------------------------------
DESIRED BASE IS ? 16

INTEGER (RADIX 10) =  ? 112234
----------------------------------------

 112234  RADIX 10 =  1 B 6  6 A BASE  16

----------------------------------------
DESIRED BASE IS ? STOP
 *TERMINATED*
```

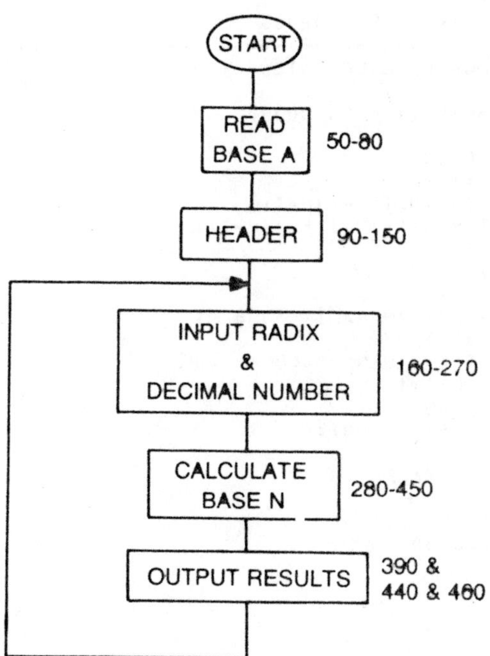

Base Conversion

PROGRAM

```
00010 PRINT
00020 REM CHANGING BASES
00030 REM KT APRIL 1978
00040 DIM D(20), N(20)
00050 FOR J=1 TO 6
00060 READ D$(J)
00070 NEXT J
00080 DATA A,B,C,D,E,F
00090 PRINT"              CHANGING BASES"
00100 PRINT"              --------------"
00110 PRINT
00120 PRINT"THIS PROGRAM ACCEPTS A POSITIVE INTEGER"
00130 PRINT"IN BASE 10 (RADIX 10), AND WILL CONVERT IT"
00140 PRINT"TO ANY BASE FROM 2 TO 16"
00150 PRINT
00160 PRINT"-------------------------------------------"
00170 PRINT"DESIRED BASE IS ";
00180 INPUT B
00190 IF B<2 THEN 00170
00200 IF B>16 THEN 00170
00210 IF B-INT(B)>0 THEN 00170
00220 PRINT
00230 PRINT"INTEGER (RADIX 10) = ";
00240 INPUT N(1)
00250 IF N(1)-INT(N(1))>0 THEN 00230
```

```
00260 IF N(1)<0 THEN 00230
00270 PRINT"--------------------------------------------"
00280 REM NOW WE CALCULATE
00290 P=0
00300 IF B^P>N(1) THEN 00330
00310 P=P+1
00320 GOTO 00300
00330 FOR I=1 TO P
00340 D(I)=INT(N(I)/B^(P-I))
00350 N(I+1)=N(I)-(D(I)*B^(P-I))
00360 NEXT I
00370 PRINT
00380 PRINT
00390 PRINT N(1);" RADIX 10 = ";
00400 FOR I=1 TO P
00410 IF D(I)>9 THEN 00440
00420 PRINT D(I);
00430 GOTO 00450
00440 PRINT D$(D(I)-9);
00450 NEXT I
00460 PRINT " BASE ";B
00470 PRINT
00480 PRINT
00490 GOTO 00160
00500 END
```

BETA TEST

The Beta Test program generates a vector of up to 500 elements with a beta (β) distribution. Beta distribution is a statistical distribution of the form:

$$dF = \frac{1}{B(\alpha,\beta)} x^{a-1}(1-x)^{\beta-1}dx$$

where $0 \leqslant x \leqslant 1$

Beta distribution is sometimes termed Pearson distribution.

```
EXAMPLE

PROGRAM   BETATST

ALPHA LEVEL(PROBABILITY BETWEEN ZERO AND ONE)
? .5
B1 LEVEL (MUST BE GREATER THAN 1)
? 7
B2 LEVEL?(GREATER THAN 1)
? 11
HOW MANY SAMPLES?(2 TO 500)
? 24
# SAMPLES    PROBABILITY{TOLERANCE}  B(BETA)1   B(BETA)2
 24           .5                      7          11
MINIMUM      MAXIMUM                 RANGE      MEDIAN
 .15537       .628815                 .473445    .326634
MEAN         STD. DEV                VARIANCE
 .353354      .488292                 .23843
```

```
PROGRAM   BETATST
V ( 1 ) = .15537
V ( 2 ) = .166769
V ( 3 ) = .201422
V ( 4 ) = .224813
V ( 5 ) = .230482
V ( 6 ) = .237609
V ( 7 ) = .257147
V ( 8 ) = .259634
V ( 9 ) = .263395
V ( 10 ) = .280527
V ( 11 ) = .319237
V ( 12 ) = .326634
V ( 13 ) = .330405
V ( 14 ) = .38302
V ( 15 ) = .410256
V ( 16 ) = .421609
V ( 17 ) = .430149
V ( 18 ) = .455816
V ( 19 ) = .460023
V ( 20 ) = .492274
V ( 21 ) = .508869
V ( 22 ) = .516161
V ( 23 ) = .52006
V ( 24 ) = .628815

ALPHA LEVEL(PROBABILITY BETWEEN ZERO AND ONE)
? .999
B1 LEVEL (MUST BE GREATER THAN 1)
? 2
B2 LEVEL?(GREATER THAN 1)
? 2
HOW MANY SAMPLES?(2 TO 500)
? 24
# SAMPLES        PROBABILITY      B(BETA)1         B(BETA
 24               .999             2                2
MINIMUM          MAXIMUM          RANGE            MEDIAN
 .039445          3.34247          3.30302          .4127
MEAN             STD. DEV         VARIANCE
 .66871           .4808            .231169


V ( 1 ) = .039445
V ( 2 ) = 4.71258E-2
V ( 3 ) = .110643
V ( 4 ) = .182771
V ( 5 ) = .198912
V ( 6 ) = .252128
V ( 7 ) = .280238
V ( 8 ) = .292586
V ( 9 ) = .325647
V ( 10 ) = .326596
V ( 11 ) = .353321
V ( 12 ) = .412742
V ( 13 ) = .415049
```

```
PROGRAM   BETATST

V ( 14 ) = .435651
V ( 15 ) = .469488
V ( 16 ) = .526962
V ( 17 ) = .62364
V ( 18 ) = .763512
V ( 19 ) = .907176
V ( 20 ) = 1.02358
V ( 21 ) = 1.19136
V ( 22 ) = 1.6652
V ( 23 ) = 1.86278
V ( 24 ) = 3.34247

ALPHA LEVEL(PROBABILITY BETWEEN ZERO AND ONE)
? .707
B1 LEVEL (MUST BE GREATER THAN 1)
? 7
B2 LEVEL?(GREATER THAN 1)
? 5
HOW MANY SAMPLES?(2 TO 500)
? 35
# SAMPLES        PROBABILITY     B(BETA)1        B(BETA)2
 35               .707            7               5
MINIMUM          MAXIMUM         RANGE           MEDIAN
 .243984          1.39997         1.15598         .617341
MEAN             STD. DEV        VARIANCE
 .666961          .478181         .228657


V ( 1 ) = .243984
V ( 2 ) = .25349
V ( 3 ) = .263098
V ( 4 ) = .298751
V ( 5 ) = .332787
V ( 6 ) = .333229
V ( 7 ) = .389619
V ( 8 ) = .392097
V ( 9 ) = .433722
V ( 10 ) = .441554
V ( 11 ) = .450679
V ( 12 ) = .465239
V ( 13 ) = .484485
V ( 14 ) = .506295
V ( 15 ) = .534688
V ( 16 ) = .555425
V ( 17 ) = .562709
V ( 18 ) = .617341
V ( 19 ) = .640971
V ( 20 ) = .653856
V ( 21 ) = .677902
V ( 22 ) = .69535
V ( 23 ) = .724535
V ( 24 ) = .743936
V ( 25 ) = .767597
V ( 26 ) = .840583
```

```
V ( 27 ) = .904806
V ( 28 ) = .998203
V ( 29 ) = 1.01687
V ( 30 ) = 1.04546
V ( 31 ) = 1.08534
V ( 32 ) = 1.14995
V ( 33 ) = 1.15399
V ( 34 ) = 1.28512
V ( 35 ) = 1.39997
```

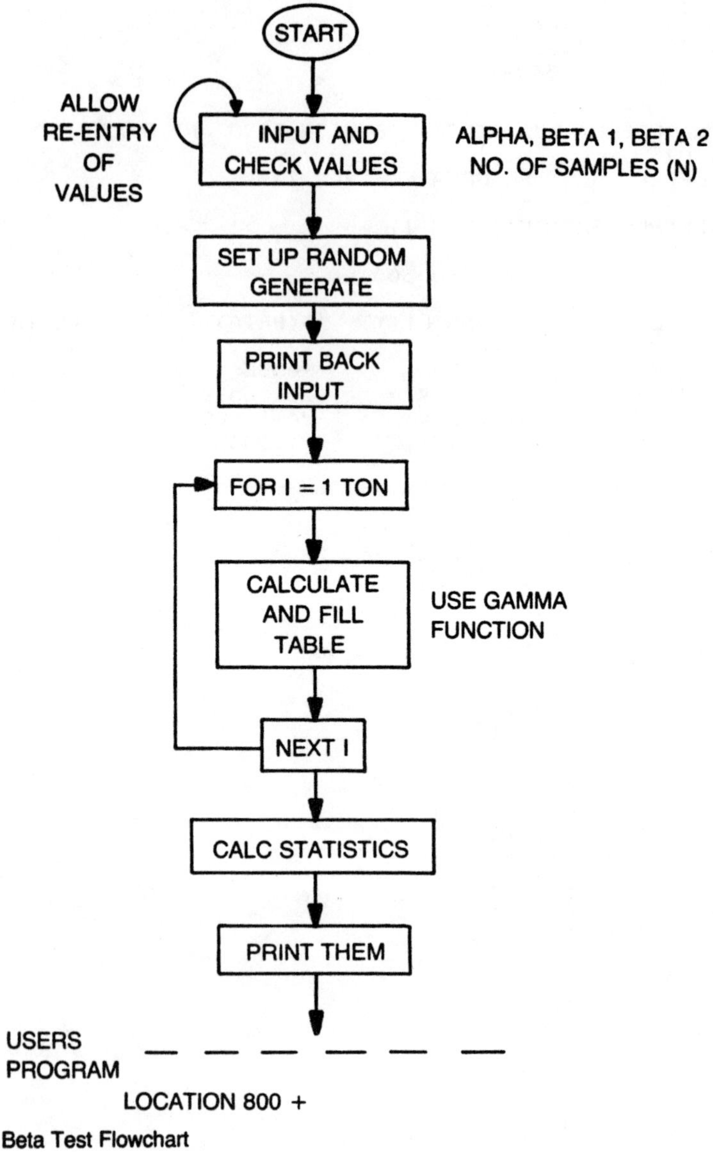

START

ALLOW RE-ENTRY OF VALUES

INPUT AND CHECK VALUES — ALPHA, BETA 1, BETA 2 NO. OF SAMPLES (N)

SET UP RANDOM GENERATE

PRINT BACK INPUT

FOR I = 1 TON

CALCULATE AND FILL TABLE — USE GAMMA FUNCTION

NEXT I

CALC STATISTICS

PRINT THEM

USERS PROGRAM

LOCATION 800 +

Beta Test Flowchart

START

FOR I = 1 TON

PRINT V (I)

NEXT I

Beta Test Sample Program

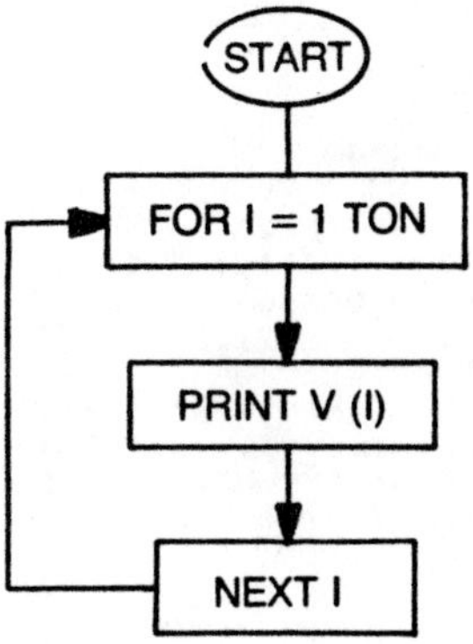

PROGRAM

```
00100 REM BETA DISTRIBUTION PROGRAM
00110 REM PLACE YOUR TEST PROGRAM AT LOCATION 800
00120 REM THE CURRENT VERSION PRINTS THE GENERATED ARRAY
00130 DIM V(500)
00140 PRINT'ALPHA LEVEL(PROBABILITY BETWEEN ZERO AND ONE)'
00150 INPUT Q4
00160 IF Q4<0 OR Q4>1 THEN 00140
00170 PRINT 'B1 LEVEL (MUST BE GREATER THAN 1)'
00180 INPUT B1
00190 B1=INT(B1)
00200 IF B1<1 THEN 00170
00210 PRINT'B2 LEVEL?(GREATER THAN 1)'
00220 INPUT B2
00230 B2=INT(B2)
00240 IF B2<1 THEN 00210
00250 PRINT 'HOW MANY SAMPLES?(2 TO 500)'
00260 INPUT N
00270 IF N>500 OR N<2 THEN 00250
00280 W9=RND(0)
00290 PRINT '# SAMPLES','PROBABILITY','B(BETA)1','B(BETA)2'
00300 PRINT N,Q4,B1,B2
00310 A=Q4
00320 W1=B1+B2
00330 FOR I=1 TO N
00340 K=B1
00350 GOSUB 00720
00360 W8=Q2
00370 K=W1
00380 GOSUB 00720
00390 V(I)=W8/Q2
00400 NEXT I
00410 REM COMPUTE STATISTICALLY SIGNIFICANT DATA AND PRINT IT
00420 REM INCLUDE MIN/MAX/MEDIAN/RANGE
00430 W5=W6=0
00440 FOR I=1 TO N
00450 W5=W5+V(I)
00460 W6=W6+V(I)
00470 NEXT I
00480 M=W5/N
00490 W7=(W6-M*W5)/(N-1)
00500 S=SQR(W7)
00510 FOR I=1 TO N
00520 FOR J=I TO N
00530 IF V(I)<=V(J) THEN 00570
```

```
00540 Q3=V(I)
00550 V(I)=V(J)
00560 V(J)=Q3
00570 NEXT J
00580 NEXT I
00590 W3=(-1)
00600 IF W3<0 THEN 00640
00610 W3=INT(N/2)
00620 B1=(V(W3)+V(W3+1))/2
00630 GOTO 00660
00640 W2=INT(N/2+.5)
00650 B1=V(W2)
00660 PRINT"MINIMUM","MAXIMUM","RANGE","MEDIAN"
00670 PRINT V(1),V(N),V(N)-V(1),B1
00680 PRINT "MEAN","STD. DEV","VARIANCE"
00690 PRINT M,S,W7
00700 GOTO 00800
00710 RETURN
00720 REM GAMMA GENERATE SUBROUTINE
00730 Q1=1
00740 FOR L=1 TO K
00750 W9=RND(0)
00760 Q1=Q1*W9
00770 NEXT L
00780 Q2=-LOG(Q1)/A
00790 RETURN
00800 REM PLACE YOUR PROGRAM HERE
00810 PRINT
00820 PRINT
00830 FOR I=1 TO N
00840 PRINT "V (";I;") =";V(I)
00850 NEXT I
00860 END
```

BIAS FOR CLASS A TRANSISTOR AMP

This program calculates the biasing network for a class A transistor amplifier through the use of an iterative technique with optimization. Then it prints an exact mathematical model and converts to EIA standard values.

Equations

1 $\Theta_{MA} = T_{J(MAX)} - 25°C/P_O$

2 $R_{L(N)} = \Theta_{JA} V_{CC}^2/44(T_{J(MAX} - T_{A(MAX)})$

3 $\longrightarrow 3$

4 If $V_{BEX} > V_{BEN}$ THEN INCREMENT R_L by $10\% \longrightarrow 3$

5 $R_{E(N)} = 0.1R_L$

6 $I_{CO} = V_{CC}/2(R_L + R_E)$

7 $I_{C(MAX)} = I_{CQ}(1 + \Delta I_{CQ})$

8 $I_{C(MIN)} = I_{CQ}(1 - \Delta I_{CQ})$

9 $T_{MAX} = \Theta_{JA} I_{CQ}(V_{CC}/2) + T_{A(MAX)}$

10 $V_{BEX} = V_{BEI(MIN)} + \Delta_{BE}\log(I_{C(MAX)}/I_1) - 0.002\ (T_{MAX} - 25)$

11 $T_{MIN} = \Theta_{JA} I_{CQ}(V_{CC}/2)(1 - \Delta I_{CQ}^2) + T_{A(MIN)}$

12 $V_{BEN} = V_{BEI(MAX)} + \Delta V_{BE}\log(I_{C(MIN)}/I_1) - 0.0022\ (T_{MIN} - 25)$

13 $R_{E(N+1)} = -2(V_{BEX} - V_{BEN})/I_{C(MAX)} - I_{C(MIN)}$

14 IF $R_{E(N+1)} - R_{E(N)}/R_{E(N)} < 0.005$ THEN $\longrightarrow$ 15

15 IF $T_{MAX} > T_{J(MAX)}$ INCREMENT R_L BY 10%

16 $R_B = \dfrac{h_{FE(MAX)} h_{FE(MIN)} R_{E(N+1)} (I_{C(MAX)} - I_{C(MIN)}) + V_{BEX} - V_{BEN}}{h_{FE(MAX)} I_{C(MIN)} - h_{FE(MIN)} I_{C(MAX)}}$

17 $V_{BB} = V_{BEN} + I_{C(MIN)}(R_E/h_{FE(MIN)} + R_{E(N+1)})$

18 $R_1 = R_B V_{CC}/V_{BB}$
19 $R_2 = R_B V_{CC}/V_{CC} - V_{BB}$

20 $A_P = R_B R_L h_{FE(MIN)}/R_{E(N+1)} R_B + h_{FE(MIN)} R_{E(N+1)}$

21 $P_S = (1 - \Delta I_{CQ})^2 \left(\dfrac{(V_{CC}^2 R_L}{8(R_L + R_{E(N+1)})} \right)^2$

where

ΔI_{CQ}	variation & quiescent current
$T_{A(MAX)}$	maximum ambient temperature
$T_{A(MIN)}$	minimum ambient temperature
$T_{J(MAX)}$	maximum allowable junction temperature
P_D	rated power dissipation at 25°C
I_1	collector current
ΔV_{BE}	base-emitter voltage change
$V_{BE1(MIN)}$	minimum base-emitter voltage
$V_{BEI(MAX)}$	maximum base-emitter voltage
$h_{FE(MAX)}$	maximum current gain
$h_{FE(MIN)}$	minimum current gain

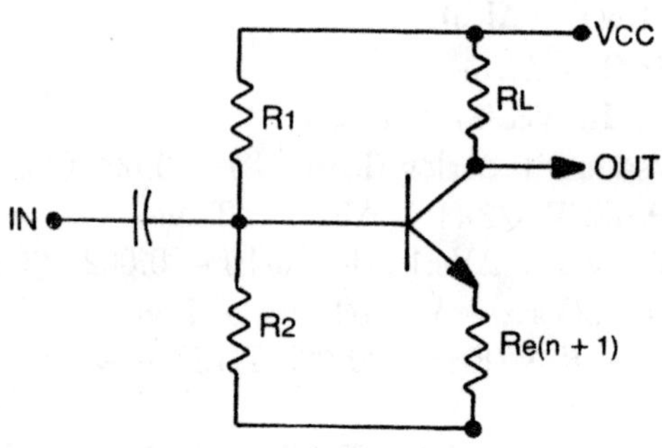

EXAMPLE

```
----------------------------------------
BIAS OPTIMIZATION OF A CLASS-A AMPLIFIER
----------------------------------------


ENTER MAXIMUM AMBIENT TEMPERATURE (USE CASE TEMP WITH HEAT SINKS)

? 70

ENTER MINIMUM AMBIENT TEMPERATURE

? 0

ENTER MAXIMUM JUNCTION TEMPERATURE RATING

? 150

ENTER MAXIMUM RATED POWER DISSIPATION AT 25C

? 0.36

ENTER COLLECTOR CURRENT, SELECTED SUCH THAT I AND
10I BRACKET THE EXPECTED OPERATING POINT

? 5E-03

ENTER TYPICAL BASE-EMITTER VOLTAGE CHANGE OVER THE
RANGE OF I TO 10I AT 25C

? .1

ENTER TYPICAL MINIMUM BASE-EMITTER VOLTAGE AT I (25C)

? .52

ENTER TYPICAL MAXIMUM BASE-EMITTER VOLTAGE AT I (25C)

? .72

ENTER MAXIMUM WORST CASE CURRENT GAIN AT T-MAX

? 600

ENTER MINIMUM WORST CASE CURRENT GAIN AT T-MIN

? 100

ENTER POWER SUPPLY VOLTAGE (VCC) IN VOLTS

? 30
********************************************************
THE FOLLOWING IS AN EXACT MODEL OF THE DESIRED CIRCUIT
ALL RESISTORS ARE ROUNDED AND ARE NOT EIA STANDARDS

BIAS RESISTOR R1 =  87057  OHMS

BIAS RESISTOR R2 =  5605  OHMS

COLLECTOR/LOAD RESISTOR R3 =  887  OHMS

EMITTER RESISTOR R4 =  63  OHMS

MAXIMUM OPERATING TEMPERATURE IS  150  DEGREES C

MINIMUM OPERATING TEMPERATURE IS  70  DEGREES C

MAXIMUM COLLECTOR CURRENT IS  .020736  AMPERES
```

```
MINIMUM COLLECTOR CURRENT IS  .009984  AMPERES

MINIMUM POWER GAIN IS  626

MINIMUM SIGNAL POWER IS  4.65856E-2

********************************************************

THE FOLLOWING VALUES ARE BASED ON
EIA STANDARD RESISTORS

BIAS RESISTOR R1 =  100000  OHMS

BIAS RESISTOR R2 =  5600  OHMS

COLLECTOR/LOAD RESISTOR R3 =  1000  OHMS

EMITTER RESISTOR R4 =  68  OHMS

MAXIMUM OPERATING TEMPERATURE IS  143.151  DEGREES C

MINIMUM OPERATING TEMPERATURE IS  64.1898  DEGREES C

MAXIMUM COLLECTOR CURRENT IS  1.89607E-2  AMPERES

MINIMUM COLLECTOR CURRENT IS  9.12921E-3  AMPERES

MINIMUM POWER GAIN IS  655

MINIMUM SIGNAL POWER IS  4.16713E-2

********************************************************

SRU       0.946 UNTS.

RUN COMPLETE.
RUN
```

START
INPUT PARAMETERS
CAL VARIABLES
T
TEST
VBEX
RL = 1.1RL
F
CAL
RE(n + 1)
F
TEST
RE(N+1)
T
T
TEST
TMAX
RL = 1.1 RL
F
CAL BIAS
OUT RESULTS
(MATHEMATICAL)
CONVERT TO EIA
RECALCULATE
EFFORTS
OUT RESULTS
(ELECTRONIC)
END

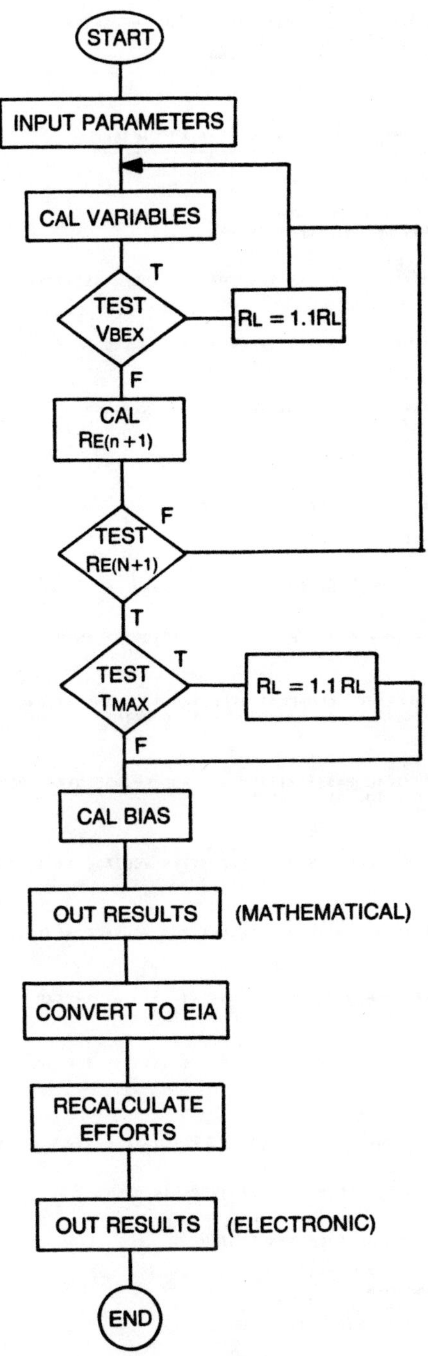

Bias

PROGRAM

```
00100 REM OPTIMIZATION OF A CLASS-A TRANSISTOR AMPLIFIER
00200 REM THIS PROGRAM DETERMINES VIA AN ITERATIVE TECHNIQUE THE
00300 REM OPTIMUM VALUES FOR R1 R2 RE AND RL
00400 PRINT
00500 PRINT
00600 PRINT
00700 PRINT"--------------------------------------"
00800 PRINT"BIAS OPTIMIZATION OF A CLASS-A AMPLIFIER"
00900 PRINT"--------------------------------------"
01000 PRINT
01100 PRINT
01200 PRINT
01300 REM KEN TRACTON 9 MARCH 1978
01400 REM % VARIATION OF QUIESCENT CURRENT
01500 A=.35
01600 REM INPUT PARAMETERS
01700 PRINT"ENTER MAXIMUM AMBIENT TEMPERATURE (USE CASE TEMP WITH HEAT SINKS)"
01800 PRINT
01900 INPUT B
02000 PRINT
02100 PRINT"ENTER MINIMUM AMBIENT TEMPERATURE"
02200 PRINT
02300 INPUT C
02400 PRINT
02500 PRINT"ENTER MAXIMUM JUNCTION TEMPERATURE RATING"
02600 PRINT
02700 INPUT D
02800 REM T(J)MAX >25C
02900 IF D<=25 THEN 03100
03000 GOTO 03400
03100 PRINT"T(J)MAX MUST BE GREATER THAN 25C"
03200 GOTO 02500
03300 REM T(J)MAX >T(A)MAX
03400 IF D<B THEN 03600
03500 GOTO 03800
03600 PRINT"T(J)MAX MUST BE GREATER THAN T(A)MAX"
03700 GOTO 02500
03800 PRINT
03900 PRINT"ENTER MAXIMUM RATED POWER DISSIPATION AT 25C"
04000 PRINT
04100 INPUT E
04200 PRINT
04300 PRINT"ENTER COLLECTOR CURRENT, SELECTED SUCH THAT I AND "
04400 PRINT"10I BRACKET THE EXPECTED OPERATING POINT"
04500 PRINT
04600 INPUT F
04700 PRINT
04800 PRINT"ENTER TYPICAL BASE-EMITTER VOLTAGE CHANGE OVER THE"
04900 PRINT"RANGE OF I TO 10I AT 25C"
05000 PRINT
05100 INPUT G
05200 PRINT
05300 PRINT"ENTER TYPICAL MINIMUM BASE-EMITTER VOLTAGE AT I (25C)"
05400 PRINT
05500 INPUT H
05600 PRINT
05700 PRINT"ENTER TYPICAL MAXIMUM BASE-EMITTER VOLTAGE AT I (25C)"
05800 PRINT
05900 INPUT I
06000 PRINT
06100 PRINT"ENTER MAXIMUM WORST CASE CURRENT GAIN AT T-MAX"
06200 PRINT
06300 INPUT X3
06400 PRINT
06500 PRINT"ENTER MINIMUM WORST CASE CURRENT GAIN AT T-MIN"
06600 PRINT
06700 INPUT X4
06800 IF X4>=X3 THEN 07000
06900 GOTO 07200
07000 PRINT"MINIMUM CURRENT GAIN MUST BE LESS THEN MAXIMUM CURRENT GAIN"
07100 GOTO 06000
07200 PRINT
07300 PRINT"ENTER POWER SUPPLY VOLTAGE (VCC) IN VOLTS"
07400 PRINT
07500 INPUT J
07600 REM THERMAL RESISTANCE OF TRANSISTOR
07700 K=(D-25)/E
07800 REM MINIMUM LOAD RESISTANCE
07900 L=(K*J^2)/(4.4*(D-B))
08000 REM EMITTER RESISTANCE
08100 REM ENTRY POINT TO ITERATIVE LOOP
08200 M=0.1*L
```

```
08300 REM QUIESCENT CURRENT
08400 N=J/(2*(L+M))
08500 REM MAXIMUM COLLECTOR CURRENT
08600 P=N*(1+A)
08700 REM MINIMUM COLLECTOR CURRENT
08800 Q=N*(1-A)
08900 REM T-MAX
09000 R=K*N*(J/2)+B
09100 REM VBEX
09200 S=H+(G*(LOG(P/F)/LOG(10)))-(0.0022*(R-25))
09300 REM T-MIN
09400 T=K*N*(J/2)*(1-A^2)+C
09500 REM VBEN
09600 U=I+(G*(LOG(Q/F)/LOG(10)))-(0.0022*(T-25))
09700 IF S>U THEN 11100
09800 V=(-2*(S-U))/(P-Q)
09900 IF ((V-M)/M)<0.005 THEN 10100
10000 GOTO 11200
10100 IF R>D THEN 11400
10200 X1=(X3*X4*((V*(P-Q))+S-U))/(X3*Q-X4*P)
10300 X2=U+(Q*(X1/X4+V))
10400 REM BIAS RESISTOR R1
10500 W=(X1*J)/X2
10600 REM BIAS RESISTOR R2
10700 X=(X1*J)/(J-X2)
10800 Z=(X1*L*X4)/(V*(X1+X4*V))
10900 O=((1-A)^2)*(((J^2)*L)/(8*((L+V)^2)))
11000 GOTO 12000
11100 M=0
11200 L=1.1*L
11300 GOTO 08200
11400 L=1.1*L
11500 GOTO 10200
11600 REM OUTPUT RESULTS
11700 REM THESE RESULTS ARE AN EXACT SOLUTION (MATHEMATICAL)
11800 PRINT
11900 PRINT
12000 PRINT"***************************************************************"
12100 PRINT
12200 PRINT"THE FOLLOWING IS AN EXACT MODEL OF THE DESIRED CIRCUIT"
12300 PRINT"ALL RESISTORS ARE ROUNDED AND ARE NOT EIA STANDARDS"
12400 PRINT
12500 W=INT(W)
12600 PRINT"BIAS RESISTOR R1 = ";W;" OHMS"
12700 PRINT
12800 X=INT(X)
12900 PRINT"BIAS RESISTOR R2 = ";X;" OHMS"
13000 PRINT
13100 L=INT(L)
13200 PRINT"COLLECTOR/LOAD RESISTOR R3 = ";L;" OHMS"
13300 PRINT
13400 V=INT(V)
13500 PRINT"EMITTER RESISTOR R4 = ";V;" OHMS"
13600 PRINT
13700 R=INT(R)
13800 PRINT"MAXIMUM OPERATING TEMPERATURE IS ";R;" DEGREES C"
13900 PRINT
14000 T=INT(T)
14100 PRINT"MINIMUM OPERATING TEMPERATURE IS ";T;" DEGREES C"
14200 PRINT
14300 PRINT"MAXIMUM COLLECTOR CURRENT IS ";P;" AMPERES"
14400 PRINT
14500 PRINT"MINIMUM COLLECTOR CURRENT IS ";Q;" AMPERES"
14600 PRINT
14700 Z=INT(Z)
14800 PRINT"MINIMUM POWER GAIN IS ";Z
14900 PRINT
15000 PRINT"MINIMUM SIGNAL POWER IS ";O
15100 PRINT
15200 PRINT"***************************************************************"
15300 REM THIS SOLUTION IS AN ELECTRONIC SOLUTION DERIVED
15400 REM BY USING EIA STANDARD RESISTORS AND RE-OPTIMIZING
15500 GOSUB 22400
15600 N=J/(2*(L+V))
15700 P=N*(1+A)
15800 Q=N*(1-A)
15900 R=K*N*(J/2)+B
16000 S=H+(G*(LOG(P/F)/LOG(10)))-(0.0022*(R-25))
16100 T=K*N*(J/2)*(1-A^2)+C
16200 U=I+(G*(LOG(Q/F)/LOG(10)))-(0.0022*(T-25))
16300 X1=(X3*X4*((V*(P-Q))+S-U))/(X3*Q-X4*P)
16400 X2=U+(Q*(X1/X4+V))
16500 W=(X1*J)/X2
16600 X=(X1*J)/(J-X2)
16700 Z=(X1*L*X4)/(V*(X1+X4*V))
16800 O=((1-A)^2)*(((J^2)*L)/(8*((L+V)^2)))
```

```
16900 GOSUB 19900
17000 PRINT
17100 PRINT"THE FOLLOWING VALUES ARE BASED ON"
17200 PRINT"EIA STANDARD RESISTORS "
17300 PRINT
17400 PRINT"BIAS RESISTOR R1 = ";W;" OHMS"
17500 PRINT
17600 PRINT"BIAS RESISTOR R2 = ";X;" OHMS"
17700 PRINT
17800 PRINT"COLLECTOR/LOAD RESISTOR R3 = ";L;" OHMS"
17900 PRINT
18000 PRINT"EMITTER RESISTOR R4 = ";V;" OHMS"
18100 PRINT
18200 PRINT"MAXIMUM OPERATING TEMPERATURE IS ";R;" DEGREES C"
18300 PRINT
18400 PRINT"MINIMUM OPERATING TEMPERATURE IS ";T;" DEGREES C"
18500 PRINT
18600 PRINT"MAXIMUM COLLECTOR CURRENT IS ";P;" AMPERES"
18700 PRINT
18800 PRINT"MINIMUM COLLECTOR CURRENT IS ";C;" AMPERES"
18900 PRINT
19000 Z=INT(Z)
19100 PRINT"MINIMUM POWER GAIN IS ";Z
19200 PRINT
19300 PRINT"MINIMUM SIGNAL POWER IS ";O
19400 PRINT
19500 PRINT"**************************************************************"
19600 REM NOW WE ARE FINISHED
19700 STOP
19800 REM EIA STANDARD FOR R1
19900 RESTORE
20000 READ L1
20100 IF W>L1 THEN 20300
20200 GOTO 20500
20300 L2=L1
20400 GOTO 20000
20500 IF ABS(L1-W) >= ABS(L2-W) THEN 20700
20600 GOTO 20900
20700 W=L2
20800 GOTO 21100
20900 W=L1
21000 REM EIA STANDARD FOR R2
21100 RESTORE
21200 READ L1
21300 IF X>L1 THEN 21500
21400 GOTO 21700
21500 L2=L1
21600 GOTO 21200
21700 IF ABS(L1-X) >= ABS(L2-X) THEN 21900
21800 GOTO 22100
21900 X=L2
22000 GOTO 22400
22100 X=L1
22200 RETURN
22300 REM EIA STANDARD FOR R3
22400 RESTORE
22500 READ L1
22600 IF L>L1 THEN 22500
22700 L=L1
22800 L2=L1
22900 REM EIA STANDARD FOR R4
23000 RESTORE
23100 READ L1
23200 IF V>L1 THEN 23100
23300 V=L1
23400 RETURN
23500 DATA 1,1.2,1.5,1.8,2.2,2.7
23600 DATA 3.3,3.9,4.7,5.6,6.8
23700 DATA 8.2,10,12,15,18,22,27,
23800 DATA 33,39,47,56,68,82,100
23900 DATA 120,150,180,220,270,330
24000 DATA 390,470,560,680,820,1000
24100 DATA 1200,1500,1800,2200,2700
24200 DATA 3300,3900,4700,5600,6800
24300 DATA 8200,1E04,1.2E04,1.5E04
24400 DATA 1.8E04,2.2E04,2.7E04,3.3E04
24500 DATA 3.9E04,4.7E04,5.6E04,6.8E04
24600 DATA 8.2E04,1E05,1.2E05,1.5E05
24700 DATA 1.8E05,2.2E05,2.7E05,3.3E05
24800 DATA 3.9E05,4.7E05,5.6E05,6.8E05
24900 DATA 8.2E05,1E06,1.2E06,1.5E06,
25000 DATA 1.8E06,2.2E06,2.7E06,3.3E06
25100 DATA 3.9E06,4.7E06,5.6E06,6.8E06,8.2E06
25200 DATA 1E07
25300 END
```

CAPACITANCE IN PARALLEL AND SERIES

This program will compute either parallel or series impedance for up to 100 capacitors.

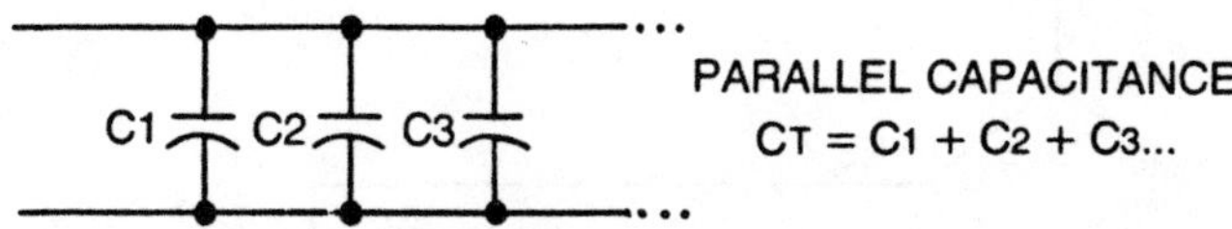

C1 C2 C3 C4

SERIES CAPACITANCE

$C_T = 1/1/C_1 + 1/C_2 + 1/C_3...$

```
EXAMPLE

RUN

TYPE 1 FOR PARALLEL, 2 FOR SERIES

? 1

HOW MANY CAPACITORS

? 2

CAPACITOR 1 = 10

CAPACITOR 2 = 15
```

```
TOTAL PARALLEL CAPACITANCE = 25 MFDS
TYPE 1 FOR PARALLEL, 2 FOR SERIES
? 2
HOW MANY CAPACITORS
? 2
CAPACITOR 1 = 10
CAPACITOR 2 = 10
TOTAL SERIES CAPACITANCE = 5 MFDS
///
RUN COMPLETE
```

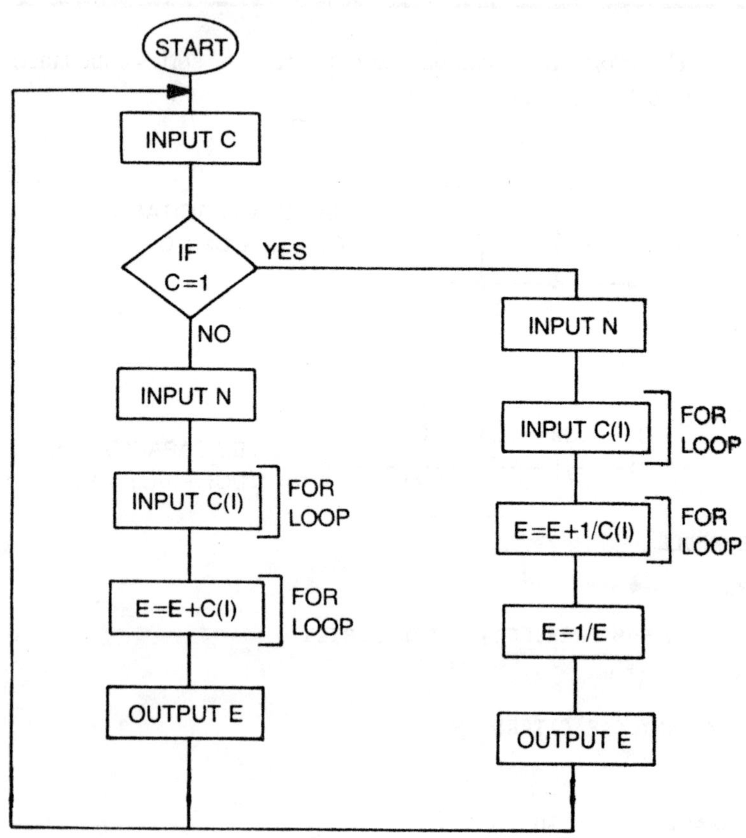

Parallel & Series Capacitance

PROGRAM

```
 10  REM THIS PROGRAM COMPUTES
 20  REM SERIES AND PARALLEL CAPACITANCE
 30  REM KT APRIL 1978
 40  DIM C{100}
 50  REM LETS GET GOING
 60  PRINT
 70  PRINT ''TYPE 1 FOR PARALLEL, 2 FOR
     SERIES''
 80  INPUT L
 90  IF C < > 1 THEN 260
100  PRINT
110  PRINT ''HOW MANY CAPACITORS''
120  INPUT N
130  FOR J = 1 TO N
140  PRINT ''CAPACITOR ''; J; ''='';
150  INPUT C{J}
160  PRINT
170  NEXT J
180  E = 0
190  FOR J = 1 TO N
200  E = E + C{J}
210  NEXT J
220  PRINT
230  PRINT ''TOTAL PARALLEL CAPACITANCE
     =''; E; ''MFDS''
240  PRINT
250  GOTO 70
260  PRINT ''HOW MANY CAPACITORS''
270  INPUT N
```

```
280  FOR J = 1 TO N
290  PRINT ''CAPACITOR''; J; ''=''; 
300  INPUT C{J}
310  PRINT
320  NEXT J
330  E = 0
340  FOR J = 1 TO N
350  E = E + {1/C{J}}
360  NEXT J
370  E = 1/E
380  PRINT
390  PRINT ''TOTAL SERIES CAPACITANCE
     = ''; E; ''MFDS''
400  PRINT
410  GOTO 70
420  END
```

CHEBYSHEV BAND-PASS FILTER

This program computes a Chebyshev Band-pass Filter. Information required for this program is as follows: load impedance, center frequency, bandwidth in hertz, the slope frequency (uses symmetrical slopes, so enter the upper slope only), the desired attenuation, and the maximum allowable ripple.

where

$T_1, T_2, \ldots T_N$ are shunt tanks

$S_2, S_4, \ldots S_{N-1}$ are series pass

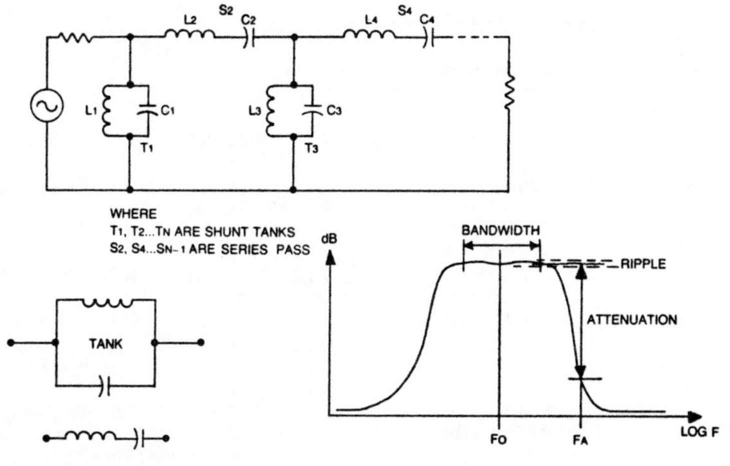

EXAMPLE

```
                 BPCHEV FILTER OPTIMIZER
*
*
ENTER THE LOAD IMPEDANCE(>0)
? 100
ENTER CENTER FREQUENCY
? 10.7E6
ENTER BANDWIDTH IN HERTZ
? 2.2E5
ENTER SLOPE FREQUENCY
? 10.91E6
ENTER THE ATTENUATION DESIRED AT  10910000
? 84
ENTER THE MAXIMUM ALLOWED RIPPLE
? 1.5
     *****************************
*
          DESIGN RESULTS FOR A
                CHEBYSHEV
                BAND-PASS
                 FILTER
*
     *****************************
*
CENTER FREQUENCY(HZ)              10700000
BANDWIDTH IN HERTZ                220000
ATTENUATION SLOPE FREQUENCY       10910000
ATTENUATION SLOPE VALUE(DB)       84
       AS A VOLTAGE RATIO         15848.9
RIPPLE OR CUTOFF PRE-RISE(DB)     1.5
RIPPLE AS A VOLTAGE RATIO         1.1885
LOAD/SOURCE IMPEDANCE             100
CALCULATED FILTER ORDER           10

*
          ********************
*
          COMPONENT VALUES
*
          ********************
*
STAGE           COMPONENT        VALUE            TYPE
--------------------------------------------------------------
*
 1              CAPACITOR        1.03682E-10      SHUNT/TANK
                INDUCTOR         2.13388E-6
 2              CAPACITOR        1.76251E-11      SERIES/PASS
                INDUCTOR         1.25529E-5
 3              CAPACITOR        3.08035E-10      SHUNT/TANK
                INDUCTOR         7.18244E-7
 4              CAPACITOR        1.07809E-11      SERIES/PASS
                INDUCTOR         2.05219E-5
 5              CAPACITOR        4.18946E-10      SHUNT/TANK
                INDUCTOR         5.28098E-7
 6              CAPACITOR        8.71699E-12      SERIES/PASS
                INDUCTOR         2.53809E-5
 7              CAPACITOR        4.87555E-10      SHUNT/TANK
                INDUCTOR         4.53784E-7
 8              CAPACITOR        7.82971E-12      SERIES/PASS
                INDUCTOR         2.82571E-5
```

```
 9          CAPACITOR        5.23938E-10    SHÜNT/TANK
            INDUCTOR         4.22273E-7
 10         CAPACITOR        7.51087E-12    SERIES/PASS
            INDUCTOR         2.94566E-5
 11         CAPACITOR        5.31182E-10    SHUNT/TANK
            INDUCTOR         4.16513E-7
 12         CAPACITOR        7.61169E-12    SERIES/PASS
            INDUCTOR         2.90664E-5
 13         CAPACITOR        5.09734E-10    SHUNT/TANK
            INDUCTOR         4.34040E-7
 14         CAPACITOR        8.17744E-12    SERIES/PASS
            INDUCTOR         2.70555E-5
 15         CAPACITOR        4.57925E-10    SHUNT/TANK
            INDUCTOR         4.83146E-7
 16         CAPACITOR        9.51629E-12    SERIES/PASS
            INDUCTOR         2.32490E-5
 17         CAPACITOR        3.70223E-10    SHUNT/TANK
            INDUCTOR         5.97599E-7
 18         CAPACITOR        1.29456E-11    SERIES/PASS
            INDUCTOR         1.70904E-5
 19         CAPACITOR        2.26385E-10    SHUNT/TANK
            INDUCTOR         9.77293E-7
*
*
********* END OF RUN *********

               BPCHEV FILTER OPTIMIZER
*
*
ENTER THE LOAD IMPEDANCE(>0)
? 1900
ENTER CENTER FREQUENCY
? 19000
ENTER BANDWIDTH IN HERTZ
? 1000
ENTER SLOPE FREQUENCY
? 20000
ENTER THE ATTENUATION DESIRED AT  20000
? 30
ENTER THE MAXIMUM ALLOWED RIPPLE
? 12
     ******************************
*
          DESIGN RESULTS FOR A
                CHEBYSHEV
                BAND-PASS
                 FILTER
*
     ******************************
*
CENTER FREQUENCY(HZ)              19000
BANDWIDTH IN HERTZ                1000
ATTENUATION SLOPE FREQUENCY       20000
ATTENUATION SLOPE VALUE(DB)       30
       AS A VOLTAGE RATIO         31.6228
RIPPLE OR CUTOFF PRE-RISE(DB)     12
RIPPLE AS A VOLTAGE RATIO         3.98107
LOAD/SOURCE IMPEDANCE             1900
CALCULATED FILTER ORDER           4
*
```

```
         ********************
*
         COMPONENT VALUES
*
         ********************
*
STAGE           COMPONENT       VALUE          TYPE
-------------------------------------------------------
*
 1              CAPACITOR        3.47618E-8     SHUNT/TANK
                INDUCTOR         2.01851E-3
 2              CAPACITOR        1.44787E-10    SERIES/PASS
                INDUCTOR         .484621
 3              CAPACITOR        7.40087E-8     SHUNT/TANK
                INDUCTOR         9.48091E-4
 4              CAPACITOR        1.19493E-10    SERIES/PASS
                INDUCTOR         .587206
 5              CAPACITOR        8.21435E-8     SHUNT/TANK
                INDUCTOR         8.54201E-4
 6              CAPACITOR        1.11209E-10    SERIES/PASS
                INDUCTOR         .630947
 7              CAPACITOR        7.48119E-8     SHUNT/TANK
                INDUCTOR         9.37912E-4
*
*
********* END OF RUN *********
                BPCHEV FILTER OPTIMIZER
*
*
ENTER THE LOAD IMPEDANCE(>0)
? 75
ENTER CENTER FREQUENCY
? 5E7
ENTER BANDWIDTH IN HERTZ
? 1E7
ENTER SLOPE FREQUENCY
? 7E7
ENTER THE ATTENUATION DESIRED AT  70000000
? 60
ENTER THE MAXIMUM ALLOWED RIPPLE
? 3
     ******************************
*
         DESIGN RESULTS FOR A
               CHEBYSHEV
               BAND-PASS
                FILTER
*
     ******************************
*
CENTER FREQUENCY(HZ)              50000000
BANDWIDTH IN HERTZ                10000000
ATTENUATION SLOPE FREQUENCY       70000000
ATTENUATION SLOPE VALUE(DB)       60
       AS A VOLTAGE RATIO         1000
RIPPLE OR CUTOFF PRE-RISE(DB)     3
RIPPLE AS A VOLTAGE RATIO         1.41254
LOAD/SOURCE IMPEDANCE             75
CALCULATED FILTER ORDER           5
*
         ********************
```

```
*
          COMPONENT VALUES
*
          ********************
*
STAGE          COMPONENT      VALUE          TYPE
-----------------------------------------------------------
*
 1            CAPACITOR      1.29819E-11    SHUNT/TANK
              INDUCTOR       7.80483E-7
 2            CAPACITOR      2.41816E-11    SERIES/PASS
              INDUCTOR       4.19001E-7
 3            CAPACITOR      3.70406E-11    SHUNT/TANK
              INDUCTOR       2.73541E-7
 4            CAPACITOR      1.59463E-11    SERIES/PASS
              INDUCTOR       6.35391E-7
 5            CAPACITOR      4.51361E-11    SHUNT/TANK
              INDUCTOR       2.24479E-7
 6            CAPACITOR      1.49846E-11    SERIES/PASS
              INDUCTOR       6.76169E-7
 7            CAPACITOR      4.26968E-11    SHUNT/TANK
              INDUCTOR       2.37304E-7
 8            CAPACITOR      1.81936E-11    SERIES/PASS
              INDUCTOR       5.56906E-7
 9            CAPACITOR      2.81236E-11    SHUNT/TANK
              INDUCTOR       3.60272E-7
*
*
********* END OF RUN *********
```

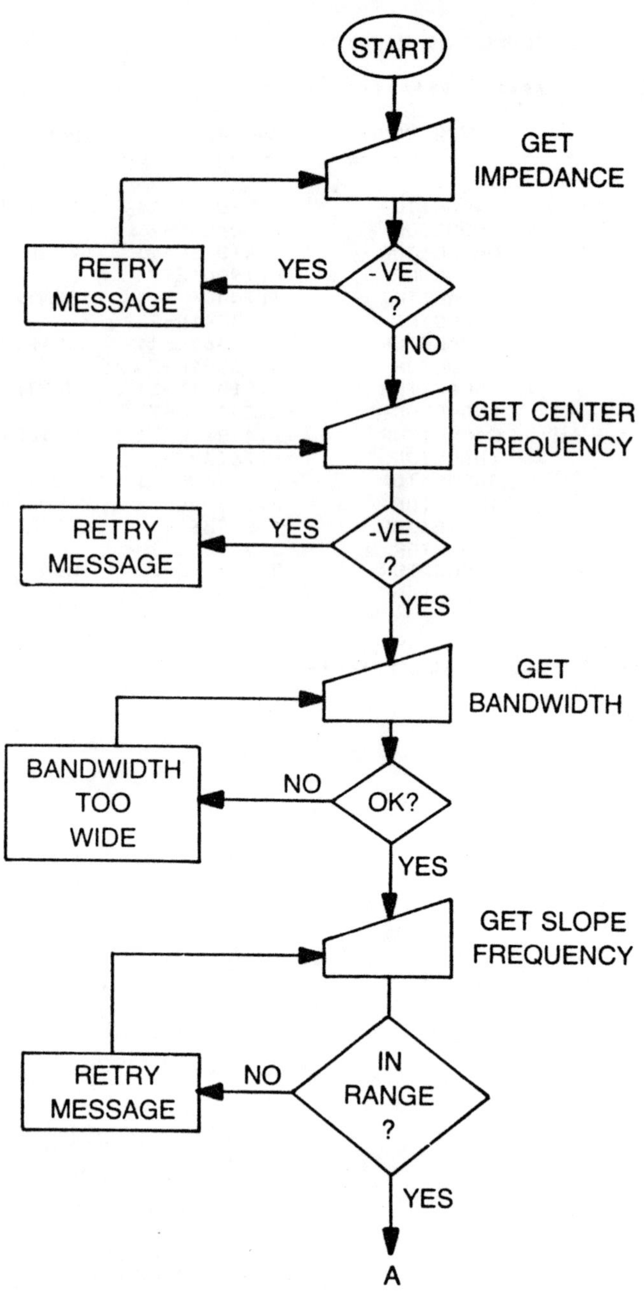

Chebyshev Band-Pass Filter

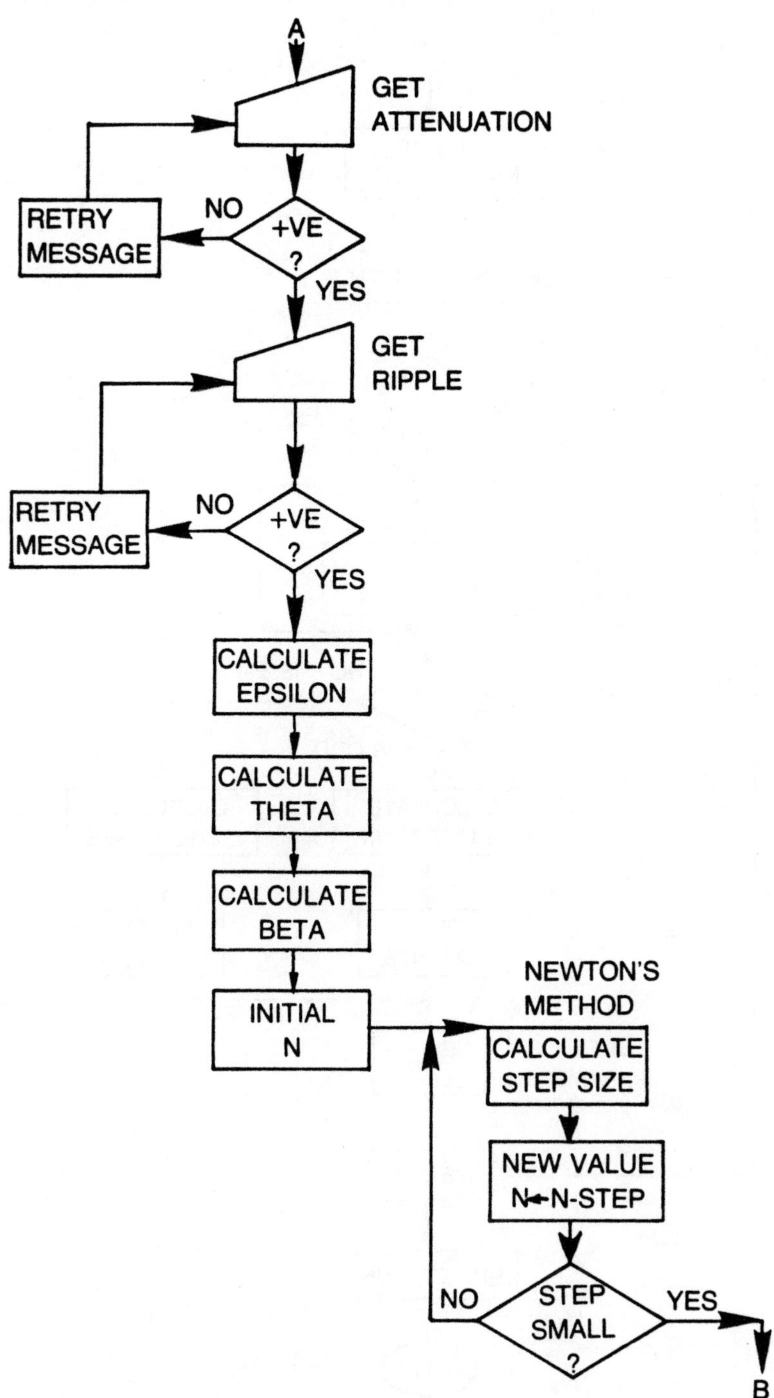
A
GET
ATTENUATION
RETRY
MESSAGE
NO
+VE
?
YES
GET
RIPPLE
RETRY
MESSAGE
NO
+VE
?
YES
CALCULATE
EPSILON
CALCULATE
THETA
CALCULATE
BETA
INITIAL
N
NEWTON'S
METHOD
CALCULATE
STEP SIZE
NEW VALUE
N←N-STEP
NO
STEP
SMALL
?
YES
B

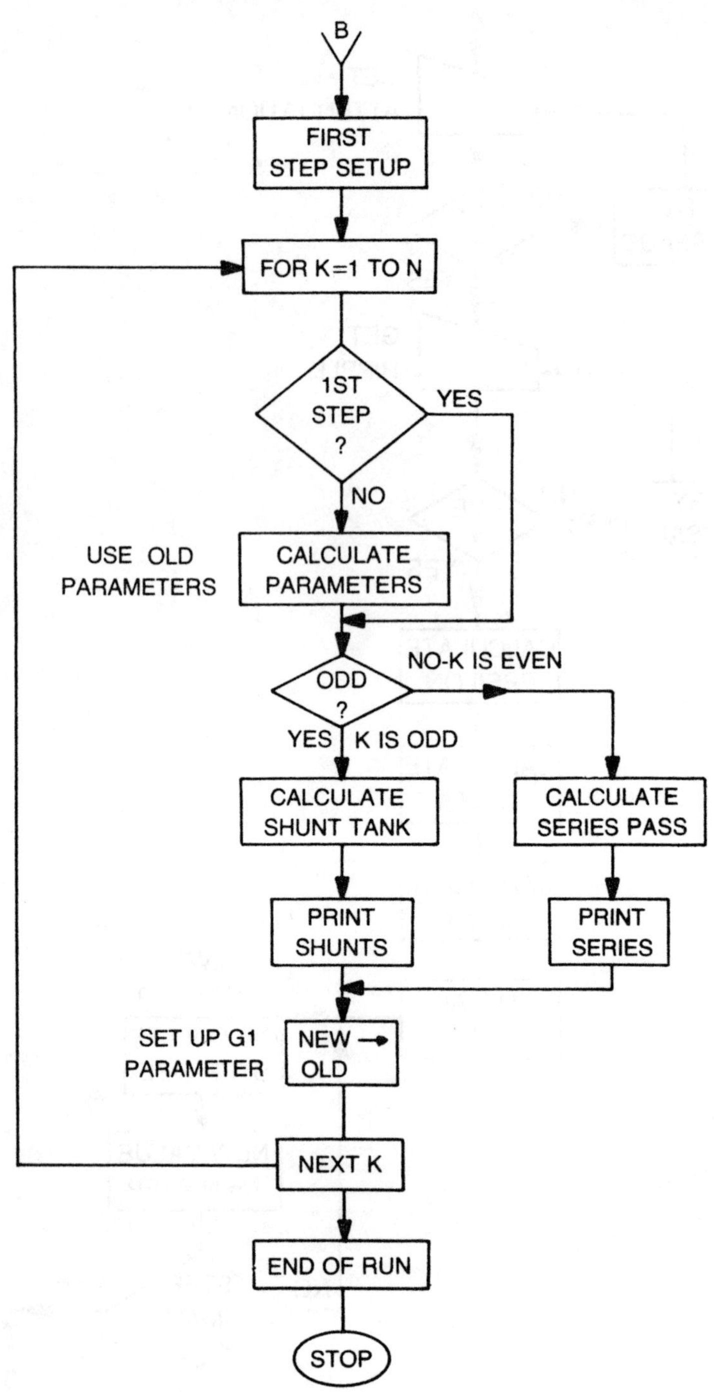
B
FIRST
STEP SETUP
FOR K=1 TO N
1ST
STEP
?
YES
NO
USE OLD
PARAMETERS
CALCULATE
PARAMETERS
NO-K IS EVEN
ODD
?
YES
K IS ODD
CALCULATE
SHUNT TANK
CALCULATE
SERIES PASS
PRINT
SHUNTS
PRINT
SERIES
SET UP G1
PARAMETER
NEW →
OLD
NEXT K
END OF RUN
STOP

```
00100 REM THIS PROGRAM DESIGNS
00200 REM A CHEBYSHEV
00300 REM BAND-PASS FILTER
00400 REM GIVEN -
00500 REM THE CENTER FREQUENCY
00600 REM THE LOAD IMPEDANCE
00700 REM THE SLOPE IN THE FORM
00800 REM OF A FREQUENCY AND
00900 REM THE ATTENUATION AT
01000 REM THE GIVEN FREQUENCY
01100 REM SINCE THE FILTER HAS A RIPPLE
01200 REM IN THE PASSED FREQUENCY
01300 REM RANGE ( IN TERMS OF "GAIN")
01400 REM THIS RIPPLE MUST BE SPECIFIED
01500 REM GET THE LOAD IMPEDANCE
01600 PRINT TAB(16);"BPCHEV FILTER OPTIMIZER"
01700 PRINT "*"
01800 PRINT "*"
01900 PRINT "ENTER THE LOAD IMPEDANCE(>0)"
02000 INPUT L1
02100 IF L1 > 0 THEN 02300
02200 GOTO 01900
02300 REM GET CENTER FREQUENCY IN HERTZ
02400 PRINT "ENTER CENTER FREQUENCY"
02500 INPUT F0
02600 IF F0 > 0 THEN 02900
02700 PRINT "FREQUENCY MUST BE POSITIVE"
02800 GOTO 02400
02900 REM GET THE BANDWIDTH
03000 PRINT "ENTER BANDWIDTH IN HERTZ"
03100 INPUT R
03200 IF R/2 < F0 THEN 03500
03300 PRINT "BANDWIDTH IS TOO WIDE"
03400 GOTO 02900
03500 REM GET THE SLOPE FREQUENCY
03600 PRINT "ENTER SLOPE FREQUENCY"
03700 INPUT F1
03800 REM CHECK FREQUENCY RANGE
03900 IF F1 >0 AND (F1<(F0-R/2) OR F1>(F0+R/2)) THEN 04200
04000 PRINT "SLOPE FREQUENCY IS INCORRECT"
04100 GOTO 03600
04200 REM GET THE SLOPE ATTENUATION IN DB
04300 PRINT "ENTER THE ATTENUATION DESIRED AT ";F1
04400 INPUT A
04500 REM CHECK THAT ATTENUATION IS VALID
04600 IF A>0 THEN 05000
04700 PRINT "ATTENUATION MUST BE >0"
04800 GOTO 04300
04900 REM GET THE RIPPLE FACTOR IN DB
05000 PRINT "ENTER THE MAXIMUM ALLOWED RIPPLE"
05100 INPUT D
05200 REM CHECK THE RIPPLE GIVEN
05300 IF D>0 THEN 05800
05400 PRINT "RIPPLE MUST BE GREATER THAN 0"
05500 GOTO 05000
05600 REM ALL THE VALUES HAVE BEEN OBTAINED
05700 REM FROM THE USER - SO WE CAN
05800 REM BEGIN THE CALCULATION PROCESS
05900 REM FIRST WE CALCULATE THE RIPPLE
06000 REM AS A FUNCTIONAL VALUE EPSILON
06100 Q=10^(D/10)
06200 E=SQR(Q/10)
06300 REM CALCULATE THE PARAMETER THETA X
06400 A1=4/(E*E)
```

```
06500 A1=A1*(10^(A/10)-1)-2
06600 REM CALCULATE THE PARAMETER BETA
06700 REM FIRST NORMALIZE THE FREQUENCIES
06800 W0=F0*6.283185307
06900 W1=F1*6.283185307
07000 W2=R*6.283185307
07100 W=(W1*W1-W0*W0)/(W2*W1)
07200 REM CONTINUE BETA CALCULATION
07300 B=SQR(W*W-1)
07400 B=W+B
07500 REM CALCULATE FIRST ESTIMATE OF N
07600 REM WHERE N IS THE NUMBER OF SHUNT
07700 REM AND SERIES GROUPS COMBINED
07800 N=LOG(A1)/LOG(B)
07900 REM WE NOW LOOP THRU THE VALUES OF N
08000 REM USING THE NEWTON METHOD FOR
08100 REM FINDING THE ROOT OF AN EQUATION
08200 REM ADJUSTING FOR THE BEST VALUE OF N
08300 REM CALCULATE THE INCREMENTAL VALUE
08400 REM USING THE EXISTING N
08500 V3=B^N
08600 V3=V3+(1/V3)-A1
08700 V4=V3-(1/V3)
08800 V5=V3/V4
08900 V7=LOG(B)*2
09000 V6=V5/V7
09100 REM ADJUST N TO THE NEW VALUE
09200 REM USING THE CORRECTION
09300 REM JUST CALCULATED (V6)
09400 N=N-V6
09500 REM IS THE CORRECTION VALUE TOO
09600 REM TO WORRY FURTHER ABOUT
09700 IF ABS(V6)>.00001 THEN 10100
09800 GOTO 08500
09900 REM ROUND UP THE VALUE TO
10000 REM THE NEXT INTEGER
10100 N=INT(N+1)
10200 REM CALCULATE THE CONSTANT ZETA
10300 Z1=D/40
10400 Z2=Z1*LOG(10)*2
10500 Y3=EXP(Z2)
10600 Y4=(Y3-1)/(Y3+1)
10700 Y5=Y4^(1/(2*N))
10800 Y6=Y4-(1/Y4)
10900 Z=(Y6*Y6)
11000 REM CALCULATE BASIC CONVERSIONS
11100 REM SHUNT CONVERSIONS
11200 REM SIN COMPONENT ADJUSTMENT
11300 N1=3.141592654/(2*N)
11400 REM COMPONENT ADJUST FOR SIN
11500 N6=2*N1
11600 REM CALCULATE THE INITIAL VALUES
11700 REM STARTING WITH A(V1)
11800 V1=SIN(N1)
11900 REM THE FIRST G VALUE (G1)
12000 G1=2*V1/(SQR(Z))
12100 REM THE FIRST B VALU^
12200 B1=SIN(N6)
12300 B1=B1*B1+Z
12400 REM BEGIN PRINTOUT RUN
12500 PRINT TAB(5);"******************************"
12600 PRINT "*"
12700 PRINT TAB(10);"DESIGN RESULTS FOR A"
12800 PRINT TAB(16); "CHEBYSHEV"
12900 PRINT TAB(16);"BAND-PASS"
```

```
13000 PRINT TAB(17);"FILTER"
13100 PRINT "*"
13200 PRINT TAB(5);"******************************"
13300 PRINT "*"
13400 PRINT "CENTER FREQUENCY(HZ)",F0
13500 PRINT "BANDWIDTH IN HERTZ",R
13600 PRINT "ATTENUATION SLOPE FREQUENCY",F1
13700 PRINT "ATTENUATION SLOPE VALUE(DB)",A
13800 PRINT "       AS A VOLTAGE RATIO",10^(A/20)
13900 PRINT "RIPPLE OR CUTOFF PRE-RISE(DB)",D
14000 PRINT "RIPPLE AS A VOLTAGE RATIO",10^(D/20)
14100 PRINT "LOAD/SOURCE IMPEDANCE",L1
14200 PRINT "CALCULATED FILTER ORDER",INT((N+1)/2)
14300 PRINT "*"
14400 PRINT TAB(10);"********************"
14500 PRINT "*"
14600 PRINT TAB(10);"COMPONENT VALUES"
14700 PRINT "*"
14800 PRINT TAB(10);"********************"
14900 PRINT "*"
15000 PRINT "STAGE","COMPONENT","VALUE","TYPE"
15100 PRINT "--------------------------------------
15200 PRINT "*"
15300 REM PRESET THE VALUES FOR THE FIRST PASS
15400 G2=G1
15500 V2=V1
15600 B2=B1
15700 REM RESULT-PRINT LOOP
15800 FOR K = 1 TO N
15900 REM IS THIS THE FIRST PASS
16000 IF K = 1 THEN 16300
16100 REM CALCULATE G2 FOR THIS PASS
16200 G2=4*V1/(B1*G1)
16300 V1=SIN((2*K-1)*N1)
16400 B1=SIN(K*N6)
16500 B1=B1*B1+Z
16600 REM IS THIS AN ODD OR EVEN PASS
16700 IF INT((K+.1)/2)*2=K THEN 17500
16800 REM THIS IS AN ODD PASS - DO SHUNT
16900 M1=G2/(L1*W2)
17000 M2=W2*L1/(W0*W0*G2)
17100 PRINT K,"CAPACITOR",M1,"SHUNT/TANK"
17200 PRINT " ","INDUCTOR",M2
17300 GOTO 17900
17400 REM EVEN PASS - DO SERIES
17500 M1=W2/(W0*W0*L1*G2)
17600 M2=L1*G2/W2
17700 PRINT K,"CAPACITOR",M1,"SERIES/PASS"
17800 PRINT " ","INDUCTOR",M2
17900 G1=G2
18000 NEXT K
18100 PRINT "*"
18200 PRINT "*"
18300 PRINT "********* END OF RUN *********"
18400 STOP
18500 END
```

CHEBYSHEV HIGH-PASS FILTER

This program derives a Chebyshev high-pass filter using the following information: slope frequency, attenuation, cutoff frequency, load impedance, and maximum allowable ripple.
L_1, L_3, L_5...L_N are shunts (inductive)
C_2, C_4,...C_{N-1} are series

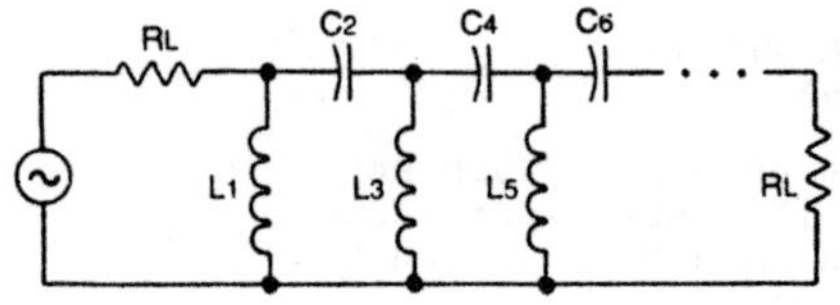

L1, L3, L5...LN ARE SHUNTS (INDUCTIVE)
C2, C4...CN-1 ARE SERIES

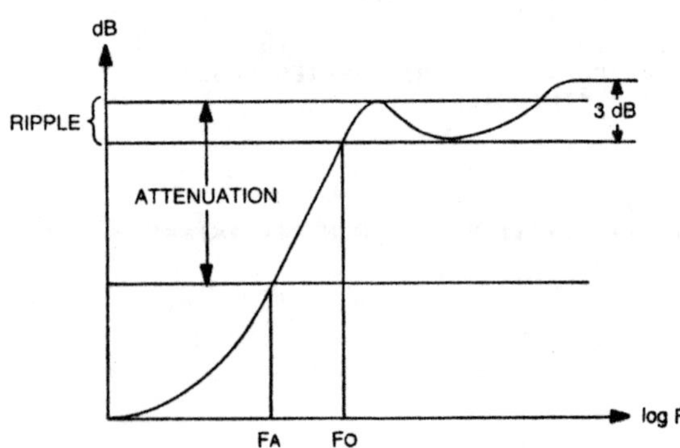

High-Pass Filter

EXAMPLE

```
*                CHEBHI FILTER OPTIMIZER
*
ENTER THE LOAD IMPEDANCE(>0)
? 1E5
ENTER FREQUENCY AT CUTOFF(3 DB DOWN)
? 1000
ENTER SLOPE FREQUENCY
? 2000
SLOPE FREQUENCY IS INCORRECT
ENTER SLOPE FREQUENCY
? 500
ENTER THE ATTENUATION DESIRED AT  500
? 84
ENTER THE MAXIMUM ALLOWED RIPPLE
? .1
     ******************************
*
          DESIGN RESULTS FOR A
                CHEBYSHEV
*               HIGHPASS
                 FILTER
*    ******************************
CUTOFF FREQUENCY(HZ)              1000
ATTENUATION SLOPE FREQUENCY       500
ATTENUATION SLOPE VALUE(DB)       84
       AS A VOLTAGE RATIO         15848.9
RIPPLE OR CUTOFF PRE-RISE(DB)     .1
RIPPLE AS A VOLTAGE RATIO         1.01158
LOAD/SOURCE IMPEDANCE             100000
CALCULATED FILTER ORDER           9
*
          ********************
*
          COMPONENT VALUES
*
          ********************
*
STAGE          COMPONENT      VALUE          TYPE
------------------------------------------------------
*
 1             INDUCTOR       15860.9        SHUNT
 2             CAPACITOR      1.38237E-7     SERIES
 3             INDUCTOR       5341.09        SHUNT
 4             CAPACITOR      8.46594E-8     SERIES
 5             INDUCTOR       3935.4         SHUNT
 6             CAPACITOR      6.86727E-8     SERIES
 7             INDUCTOR       3397.13        SHUNT
 8             CAPACITOR      6.20690E-8     SERIES
 9             INDUCTOR       3187.46        SHUNT
 10            CAPACITOR      6.01831E-8     SERIES
 11            INDUCTOR       3187.46        SHUNT
 12            CAPACITOR      6.20689E-8     SERIES
 13            INDUCTOR       3397.12        SHUNT
 14            CAPACITOR      6.86725E-8     SERIES
 15            INDUCTOR       3935.39        SHUNT
 16            CAPACITOR      8.46592E-8     SERIES
 17            INDUCTOR       5341.08        SHUNT
 18            CAPACITOR      1.38237E-7     SERIES
*
*
********* END OF RUN *********
```

```
                    CHEBHI FILTER OPTIMIZER
*
*
ENTER THE LOAD IMPEDANCE(>0)
? 50
ENTER FREQUENCY AT CUTOFF(3 DB DOWN)
? 1E6
ENTER SLOPE FREQUENCY
? 9E5
ENTER THE ATTENUATION DESIRED AT  900000
? 66
ENTER THE MAXIMUM ALLOWED RIPPLE
? 6
     *****************************
*
          DESIGN RESULTS FOR A
                CHEBYSHEV
                HIGHPASS
                 FILTER
*
     *****************************
*
CUTOFF FREQUENCY(HZ)                1000000
ATTENUATION SLOPE FREQUENCY         900000
ATTENUATION SLOPE VALUE(DB)         66
       AS A VOLTAGE RATIO           1995.26
RIPPLE OR CUTOFF PRE-RISE(DB)       6
RIPPLE AS A VOLTAGE RATIO           1.99526
LOAD/SOURCE IMPEDANCE               50
CALCULATED FILTER ORDER             19
*
          *******************
*
          COMPONENT VALUES
*
          *******************
*
STAGE           COMPONENT       VALUE           TYPE
-------------------------------------------------------
*
 1              INDUCTOR        2.57772E-4      SHUNT
 2              CAPACITOR       4.26502E-9      SERIES
 3              INDUCTOR        8.63633E-5      SHUNT
 4              CAPACITOR       2.58257E-9      SERIES
 5              INDUCTOR        6.25011E-5      SHUNT
 6              CAPACITOR       2.04278E-9      SERIES
 7              INDUCTOR        5.21900E-5      SHUNT
 8              CAPACITOR       1.76992E-9      SERIES
 9              INDUCTOR        4.64564E-5      SHUNT
 10             CAPACITOR       1.60849E-9      SERIES
 11             INDUCTOR        4.29211E-5      SHUNT
 12             CAPACITOR       1.50624E-9      SERIES
 13             INDUCTOR        4.06474E-5      SHUNT
 14             CAPACITOR       1.44015E-9      SERIES
 15             INDUCTOR        3.91865E-5      SHUNT
 16             CAPACITOR       1.39853E-9      SERIES
 17             INDUCTOR        3.83027E-5      SHUNT
 18             CAPACITOR       1.37514E-9      SERIES
 19             INDUCTOR        3.78717E-5      SHUNT
 20             CAPACITOR       1.36689E-9      SERIES
```

```
 21            INDUCTOR          3.78401E-5     SHUNT
 22            CAPACITOR         1.37287E-9     SERIES
 23            INDUCTOR          3.82097E-5     SHUNT
 24            CAPACITOR         1.39412E-9     SERIES
 25            INDUCTOR          3.90377E-5     SHUNT
 26            CAPACITOR         1.43388E-9     SERIES
 27            INDUCTOR          4.04519E-5     SHUNT
 28            CAPACITOR         1.49850E-9     SERIES
 29            INDUCTOR          4.26919E-5     SHUNT
 30            CAPACITOR         1.59980E-9     SERIES
 31            INDUCTOR          4.62097E-5     SHUNT
 32            CAPACITOR         1.76095E-9     SERIES
 33            INDUCTOR          5.19457E-5     SHUNT
 34            CAPACITOR         2.03430E-9     SERIES
 35            INDUCTOR          6.22827E-5     SHUNT
 36            CAPACITOR         2.57553E-9     SERIES
 37            INDUCTOR          8.62019E-5     SHUNT
 38            CAPACITOR         4.26096E-9     SERIES
*
*
********* END OF RUN *********
                 CHEBHI FILTER OPTIMIZER
*
*
ENTER THE LOAD IMPEDANCE(>0)
? 75
ENTER FREQUENCY AT CUTOFF(3 DB DOWN)
? 30E6
ENTER SLOPE FREQUENCY
? 15E6
ENTER THE ATTENUATION DESIRED AT  15000000
? 12
ENTER THE MAXIMUM ALLOWED RIPPLE
? 6.02
     ******************************
*
          DESIGN RESULTS FOR A
                CHEBYSHEV
                HIGHPASS
                 FILTER
*
     ******************************
*
CUTOFF FREQUENCY(HZ)             30000000
ATTENUATION SLOPE FREQUENCY      15000000
ATTENUATION SLOPE VALUE(DB)      12
       AS A VOLTAGE RATIO        3.98107
RIPPLE OR CUTOFF PRE-RISE(DB)    6.02
RIPPLE AS A VOLTAGE RATIO        1.99986
LOAD/SOURCE IMPEDANCE            75
CALCULATED FILTER ORDER          2
*
          ********************
*
          COMPONENT VALUES
*
          ********************
*
STAGE          COMPONENT       VALUE          TYPE
-------------------------------------------------------
```

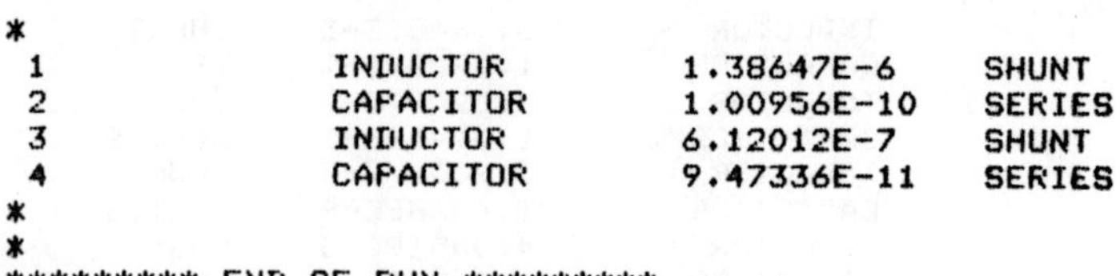

```
*
 1              INDUCTOR        1.38647E-6     SHUNT
 2              CAPACITOR       1.00956E-10    SERIES
 3              INDUCTOR        6.12012E-7     SHUNT
 4              CAPACITOR       9.47336E-11    SERIES
*
*
********* END OF RUN *********
```

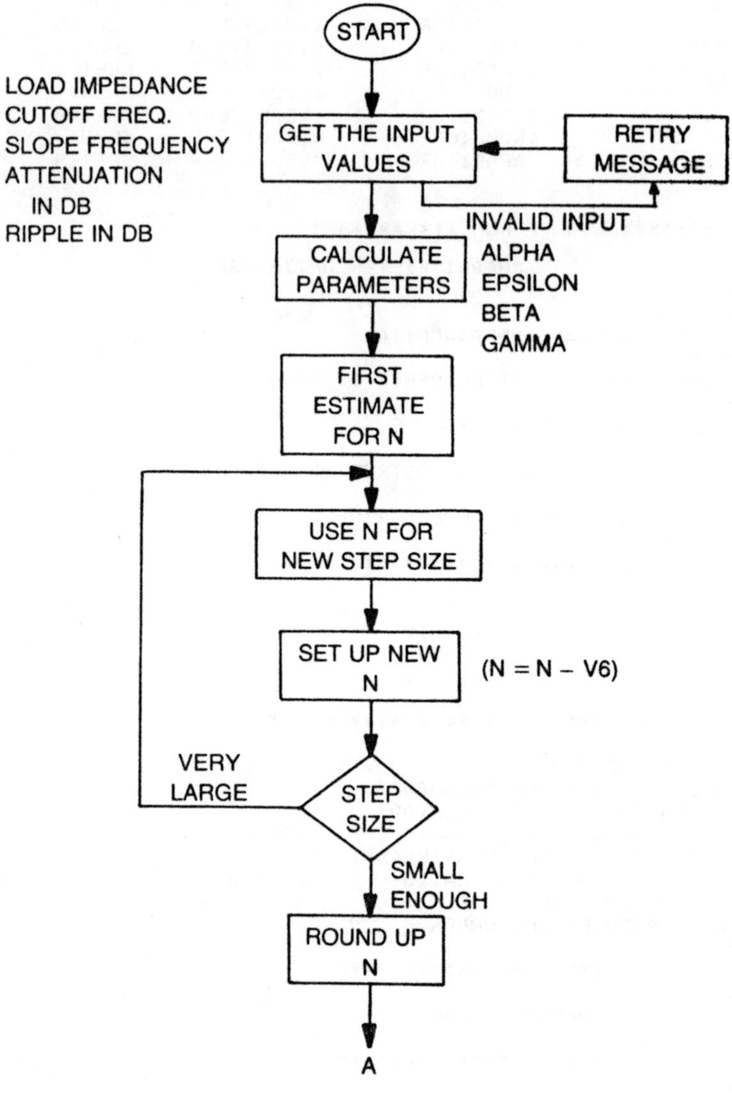

START

LOAD IMPEDANCE
CUTOFF FREQ.
SLOPE FREQUENCY
ATTENUATION
IN DB
RIPPLE IN DB

GET THE INPUT VALUES

RETRY MESSAGE

INVALID INPUT

CALCULATE PARAMETERS

ALPHA
EPSILON
BETA
GAMMA

FIRST ESTIMATE FOR N

USE N FOR NEW STEP SIZE

SET UP NEW N

(N = N – V6)

STEP SIZE

VERY LARGE

SMALL ENOUGH

ROUND UP N

A

Chebyshev High-Pass

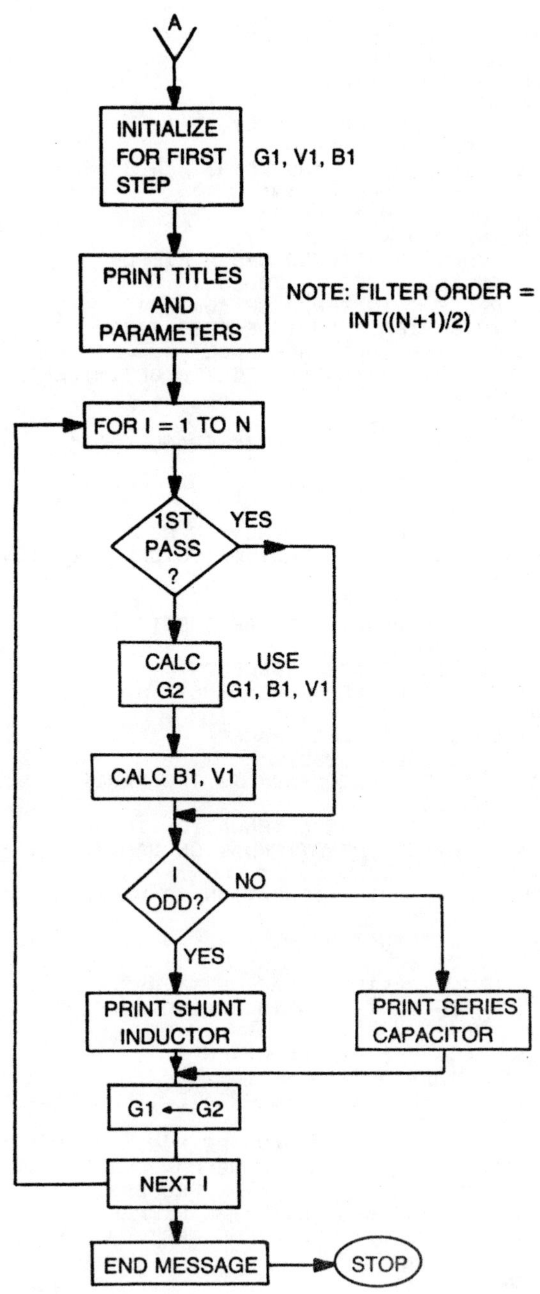

Chebyshev High-Pass

PROGRAM

```
00017 REM THIS PROGRAM DESIGNS
00024 REM A CHEBYSHEV
00031 REM HIGHPASS FILTER
00038 REM GIVEN -
00045 REM THE CUTOFF FREQUENCY
00052 REM THE LOAD IMPEDANCE
00059 REM THE SLOPE IN THE FORM
00066 REM OF A FREQUENCY AND
00073 REM THE ATTENUATION AT
00080 REM THE GIVEN FREQUENCY
00087 REM SINCE THE FILTER HAS A RIPPLE
00094 REM IN THE PASSED FREQUENCY
00101 REM RANGE ( IN TERMS OF "GAIN")
00108 REM THIS RIPPLE MUST BE SPECIFIED
00115 REM GET THE LOAD IMPEDANCE
00122 PRINT TAB(16);"CHEBHI FILTER OPTIMIZER"
00129 PRINT "*"
00136 PRINT "*"
00143 PRINT "ENTER THE LOAD IMPEDANCE(>0)"
00150 INPUT R1
00157 IF R1 > 0 THEN 00171
00164 GOTO 00143
00171 REM GET CUTOFF FREQUENCY IN HERTZ.
00178 PRINT "ENTER FREQUENCY AT CUTOFF(3 DB DOWN)"
00185 INPUT F0
00192 IF F0 > 0 THEN 00213
00199 PRINT "FREQUENCY MUST BE POSITIVE"
00206 GOTO 00178
00213 REM GET THE SLOPE FREQUENCY
00220 PRINT "ENTER SLOPE FREQUENCY"
00227 INPUT F1
00234 REM CHECK FREQUENCY RANGE
00241 IF F0>F1 THEN 00262
00248 PRINT "SLOPE FREQUENCY IS INCORRECT"
00255 GOTO 00220
00262 REM GET THE SLOPE ATTENUATION IN DB
00269 PRINT "ENTER THE ATTENUATION DESIRED AT ";F1
00276 INPUT A
00283 REM CHECK THAT ATTENUATION IS VALID
00290 IF A>0 THEN 00318
00297 PRINT "ATTENUATION MUST BE >0"
00304 GOTO 00269
00311 REM GET THE RIPPLE FACTOR IN DB
00318 PRINT "ENTER THE MAXIMUM ALLOWED RIPPLE"
00325 INPUT D
00332 REM CHECK THE RIPPLE GIVEN
00339 IF D>0 THEN 00374
00346 PRINT "RIPPLE MUST BE GREATER THAN 0"
00353 GOTO 00318
00360 REM ALL THE VALUES HAVE BEEN OBTAINED
00367 REM FROM THE USER - SO WE CAN
00374 REM BEGIN THE CALCULATION PROCESS
00381 REM FIRST WE CALCULATE THE RIPPLE
00388 REM AS A FUNCTIONAL VALUE EPSILON
00395 Q=10^(D/10)
00402 E=SQR(Q/10)
00409 REM CALCULATE THE PARAMETER ALPHA
00416 A1=4/(E*E)
00423 A1=A1*(10^(A/10)-1)-2
```

```
00430 REM CALCULATE THE PARAMETER BETA
00437 REM FIRST NORMALIZE THE FREQUENCIES
00444 W0=F0*6.283185307
00451 W1=F1*6.283185307
00458 REM CONVERT TO STANDARDIZED FORM
00465 W=W0/W1
00472 REM CONTINUE BETA CALCULATION
00479 B=SQR(W*W-1)
00486 B=W+B
00493 REM CALCULATE FIRST ESTIMATE OF N
00500 REM WHERE N IS THE NUMBER OF SHUNT
00507 REM AND SERIES GROUPS COMBINED
00514 N=LOG(A1)/LOG(B)
00521 REM WE NOW LOOP THRU THE VALUES OF N
00528 REM USING THE NEWTON METHOD FOR
00535 REM FINDING THE ROOT OF AN EQUATION
00542 REM ADJUSTING FOR THE BEST VALUE OF N
00549 REM CALCULATE THE INCREMENTAL VALUE
00556 REM USING THE EXISTING N
00563 V3=B^N
00570 V3=V3+(1/V3)-A1
00577 V4=V3-(1/V3)
00584 V5=V3/V4
00591 V7=LOG(B)*2
00598 V6=V5/V7
00605 REM ADJUST N TO THE NEW VALUE
00612 REM USING THE CORRECTION
00619 REM JUST CALCULATED (V6)
00626 N=N-V6
00633 REM IS THE CORRECTION VALUE TOO
00640 REM TO WORRY FURTHER ABOUT
00647 IF ABS(V6)>.00001 THEN 00675
00654 GOTO 00563
00661 REM ROUND UP THE VALUE TO
00668 REM THE NEXT INTEGER
00675 N=INT(N+1)
00682 REM CALCULATE THE CONSTANT GAMMA
00689 Y1=D/40
00696 Y2=Y1*LOG(10)*2
00703 Y3=EXP(Y2)
00710 Y4=(Y3-1)/(Y3+1)
00717 Y5=Y4^(1/(2*N))
00724 Y6=Y4-(1/Y4)
00731 Y=(Y6*Y6)
00738 REM CALCULATE BASIC CONVERSIONS
00745 REM SHUNT CONVERSIONS
00752 REM SIN COMPONENT ADJUSTMENT
00759 N1=3.141592654/(2*N)
00766 REM COMPONENT ADJUST FOR SIN
00773 N6=2*N1
00780 REM CALCULATE THE INITIAL VALUES
00787 REM STARTING WITH A(V1)
00794 V1=SIN(N1)
00801 REM THE FIRST G VALUE (G1)
00808 G1=2*V1/(SQR(Y))
00815 REM THE FIRST B VALUE
00822 B1=SIN(N6)
00829 B1=B1*B1+Y
00836 REM BEGIN PRINTOUT RUN
00843 PRINT TAB(5);"*******************************"
```

```
00850 PRINT "*"
00857 PRINT TAB(10);"DESIGN RESULTS FOR A"
00864 PRINT TAB(16); "CHEBYSHEV"
00871 PRINT TAB(16);"HIGHPASS"
00878 PRINT TAB(17);"FILTER"
00885 PRINT "*"
00892 PRINT TAB(5);"******************************"
00899 PRINT "*"
00906 PRINT "CUTOFF FREQUENCY(HZ)",F0
00913 PRINT "ATTENUATION SLOPE FREQUENCY",F1
00920 PRINT "ATTENUATION SLOPE VALUE(DB)",A
00927 PRINT "        AS A VOLTAGE RATIO",10^(A/20)
00934 PRINT "RIPPLE OR CUTOFF PRE-RISE(DB)",D
00941 PRINT "RIPPLE AS A VOLTAGE RATIO",10^(D/20)
00948 PRINT "LOAD/SOURCE IMPEDANCE",R1
00955 PRINT "CALCULATED FILTER ORDER",INT((N+1)/2)
00962 PRINT "*"
00969 PRINT TAB(10);"********************"
00976 PRINT "*"
00983 PRINT TAB(10);"COMPONENT VALUES"
00990 PRINT "*"
00997 PRINT TAB(10);"********************"
01004 PRINT "*"
01011 PRINT "STAGE","COMPONENT","VALUE","TYPE"
01018 PRINT "-------------------------------------
01025 PRINT "*"
01032 REM PRESET THE VALUES FOR THE FIRST PASS
01039 G2=G1
01046 V2=V1
01053 B2=B1
01060 REM RESULT-PRINT LOOP
01067 FOR I = 1 TO N
01074 REM IS THIS THE FIRST PASS
01081 IF I = 1 THEN 01102
01088 REM CALCULATE G2 FOR THIS PASS
01095 G2=4*V1/(B1*G1)
01102 V1=SIN((2*I-1)*N1)
01109 B1=SIN(I*N6)
01116 B1=B1*B1+Y
01123 REM IS THIS AN ODD OR EVEN PASS
01130 IF INT((I+.01)/2)*2=I THEN 01172
01137 REM ODD PASS - DO SHUNT
01144 M1=R1/(W0*G2)
01151 PRINT I,"INDUCTOR",M1,"SHUNT"
01158 GOTO 01186
01165 REM EVEN PASS - DO SERIES
01172 M1=1/(W0*R1*G2)
01179 PRINT I,"CAPACITOR",M1,"SERIES"
01186 G1=G2
01193 NEXT I
01200 PRINT "*"
01207 PRINT "*"
01214 PRINT "********* END OF RUN *********"
01221 STOP
01228 END
```

CHEBYSHEV LOW-PASS FILTER

This program computes a Chebyshev low-pass filter using the following information: slope frequency, attenuation, cutoff frequency, load impedance, and maximum allowable ripple.

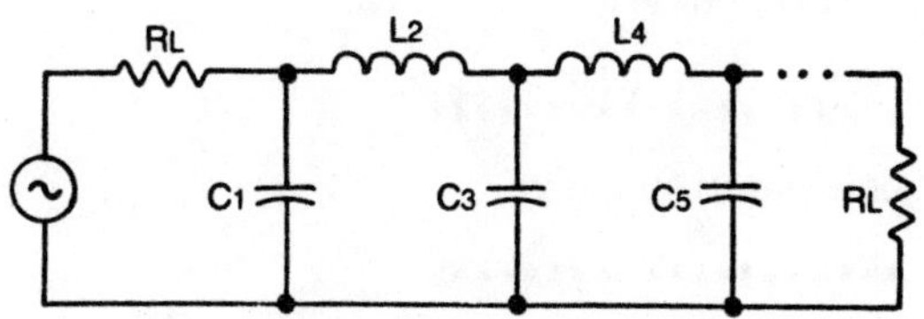

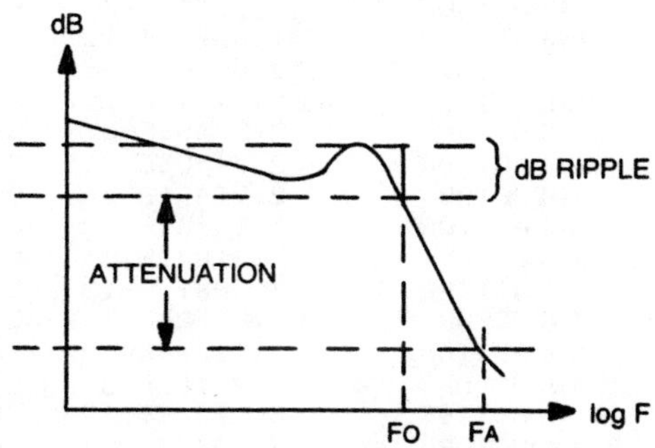

Low-Pass Filter

EXAMPLE

```
                    CHEBLO FILTER OPTIMIZER
*
*
ENTER THE LOAD IMPEDANCE(>0)
? 10000
ENTER FREQUENCY AT CUTOFF(3 DB DOWN)
? 15000
ENTER SLOPE FREQUENCY
? 19000
ENTER THE ATTENUATION DESIRED AT  19000
? 90
ENTER THE MAXIMUM ALLOWED RIPPLE
? .1
     ******************************
*
          DESIGN RESULTS FOR A
                CHEBYSHEV
                LOW-PASS
                 FILTER
*
     ******************************
*
CUTOFF FREQUENCY(HZ)              15000
ATTENUATION SLOPE FREQUENCY       19000
ATTENUATION SLOPE VALUE(DB)       90
       AS A VOLTAGE RATIO         31622.8
RIPPLE OR CUTOFF PRE-RISE(DB)     .1
RIPPLE AS A VOLTAGE RATIO         1.01158
LOAD/SOURCE IMPEDANCE             10000
CALCULATED FILTER ORDER           18
*

          ********************
*
          COMPONENT VALUES
*
          ********************
*
STAGE          COMPONENT      VALUE           TYPE
--------------------------------------------------------------
*
 1             CAPACITOR      5.48063E-13     SHUNT
 2             INDUCTOR       1.22159E-3      SERIES
 3             CAPACITOR      1.63977E-12     SHUNT
 4             INDUCTOR       2.02504E-3      SERIES
 5             CAPACITOR      2.27717E-12     SHUNT
 6             INDUCTOR       2.57556E-3      SERIES
 7             CAPACITOR      2.74556E-12     SHUNT
 8             INDUCTOR       2.99421E-3      SERIES
 9             CAPACITOR      3.10734E-12     SHUNT
 10            INDUCTOR       3.31871E-3      SERIES
 11            CAPACITOR      3.38615E-12     SHUNT
 12            INDUCTOR       3.56524E-3      SERIES
 13            CAPACITOR      3.59304E-12     SHUNT
 14            INDUCTOR       3.74183E-3      SERIES
 15            CAPACITOR      3.73367E-12     SHUNT
 16            INDUCTOR       3.85264E-3      SERIES
 17            CAPACITOR      3.81101E-12     SHUNT
```

```
 18            INDUCTOR        3.89980E-3    SERIES
 19            CAPACITOR       3.82641E-12   SHUNT
 20            INDUCTOR        3.88410E-3    SERIES
 21            CAPACITOR       3.78014E-12   SHUNT
 22            INDUCTOR        3.80529E-3    SERIES
 23            CAPACITOR       3.67141E-12   SHUNT
 24            INDUCTOR        3.66196E-3    SERIES
 25            CAPACITOR       3.49815E-12   SHUNT
 26            INDUCTOR        3.45111E-3    SERIES
 27            CAPACITOR       3.25626E-12   SHUNT
 28            INDUCTOR        3.16695E-3    SERIES
 29            CAPACITOR       2.93787E-12   SHUNT
 30            INDUCTOR        2.79823E-3    SERIES
 31            CAPACITOR       2.52709E-12   SHUNT
 32            INDUCTOR        2.32084E-3    SERIES
 33            CAPACITOR       1.98693E-12   SHUNT
 34            INDUCTOR        1.67123E-3    SERIES
 35            CAPACITOR       1.19860E-12   SHUNT
*
*
********* END OF RUN *********

               CHEBLO FILTER OPTIMIZER
*
*
ENTER THE LOAD IMPEDANCE(>0)
? 75
ENTER FREQUENCY AT CUTOFF(3 DB DOWN)
? 1.01E6
ENTER SLOPE FREQUENCY
? 0
SLOPE FREQUENCY IS INCORRECT
ENTER SLOPE FREQUENCY
? 1.5E6
ENTER THE ATTENUATION DESIRED AT  1500000
? 30
ENTER THE MAXIMUM ALLOWED RIPPLE
? 1
    ******************************
*
          DESIGN RESULTS FOR A
               CHEBYSHEV
               LOW-PASS
                FILTER
*
    ******************************
*
CUTOFF FREQUENCY(HZ)              1010000
ATTENUATION SLOPE FREQUENCY       1500000
ATTENUATION SLOPE VALUE(DB)       30
       AS A VOLTAGE RATIO         31.6228
RIPPLE OR CUTOFF PRE-RISE(DB)     1
RIPPLE AS A VOLTAGE RATIO         1.12202
LOAD/SOURCE IMPEDANCE             75
CALCULATED FILTER ORDER           6
*
          ********************
*
          COMPONENT VALUES
*
```

```
          *******************
*
STAGE              COMPONENT        VALUE            TYPE
--------------------------------------------------------------
*
 1                 CAPACITOR         3.45011E-11     SHUNT
 2                 INDUCTOR          1.36330E-6      SERIES
 3                 CAPACITOR         1.00637E-10     SHUNT
 4                 INDUCTOR          2.14711E-6      SERIES
 5                 CAPACITOR         1.29171E-10     SHUNT
 6                 INDUCTOR          2.44765E-6      SERIES
 7                 CAPACITOR         1.34624E-10     SHUNT
 8                 INDUCTOR          2.34969E-6      SERIES
 9                 CAPACITOR         1.18135E-10     SHUNT
 10                INDUCTOR          1.83078E-6      SERIES
 11                CAPACITOR         7.49927E-11     SHUNT
*
*
********* END OF RUN *********
```

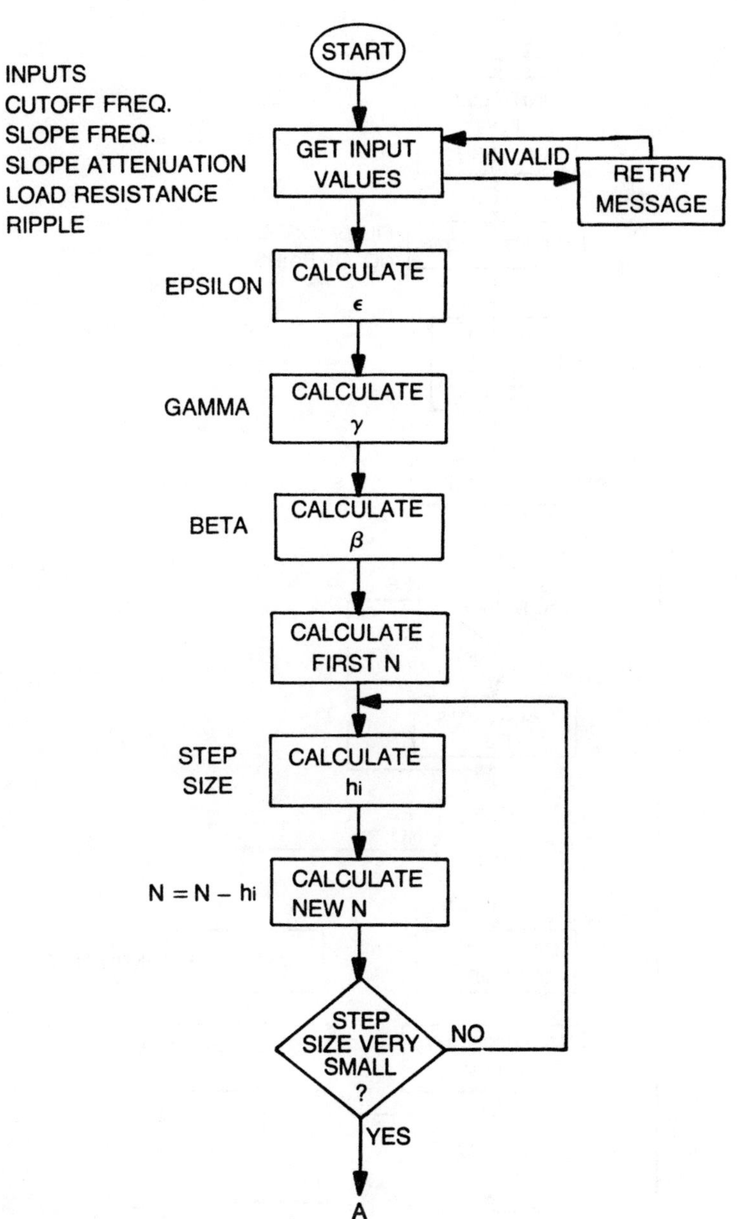

Chebychev Low-Pass

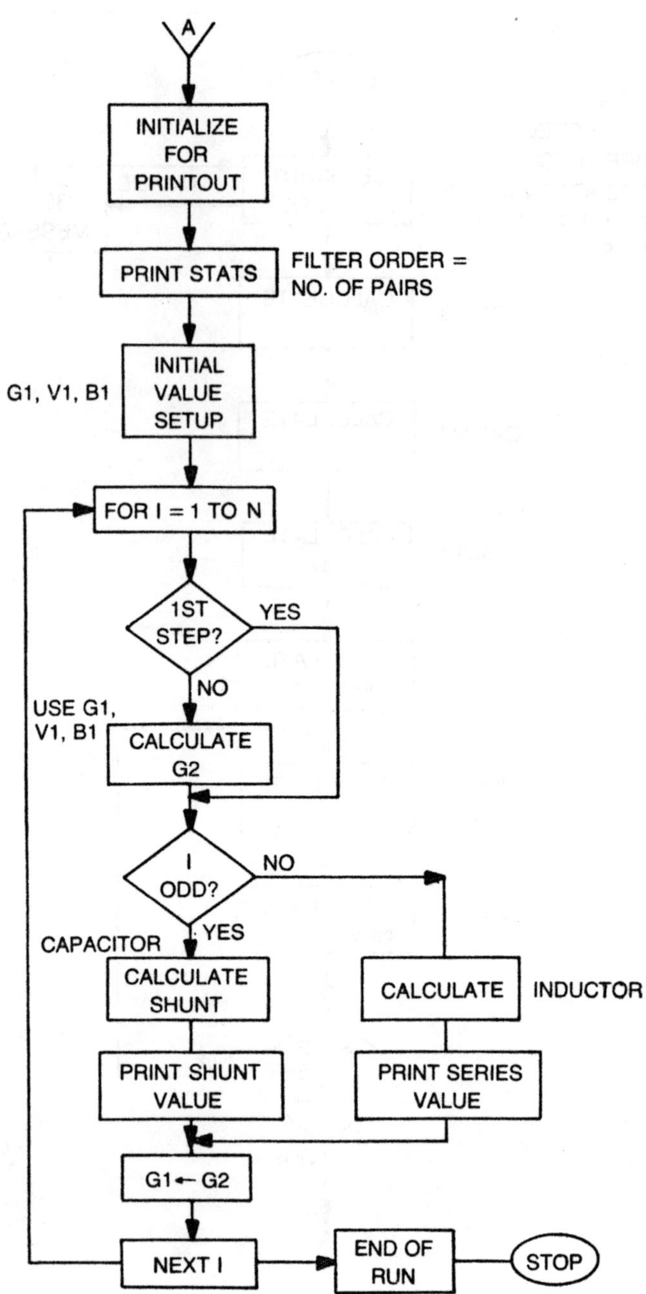

Chebychev Low-Pass

PROGRAM

```
00100 REM THIS PROGRAM DESIGNS
00110 REM A CHEBYSHEV
00120 REM LOW-PASS FILTER
00130 REM GIVEN -
00140 REM THE CUTOFF FREQUENCY
00150 REM THE LOAD IMPEDANCE
00160 REM THE SLOPE IN THE FORM
00170 REM OF A FREQUENCY AND
00180 REM THE ATTENUATION AT
00190 REM THE GIVEN FREQUENCY
00200 REM SINCE THE FILTER HAS A RIPPLE
00210 REM IN THE PASSED FREQUENCY
00220 REM RANGE ( IN TERMS OF "GAIN")
00230 REM THIS RIPPLE MUST BE SPECIFIED
00240 REM GET THE LOAD IMPEDANCE
00250 PRINT TAB(16);"CHEBLO FILTER OPTIMIZER"
00260 PRINT "*"
00270 PRINT "*"
00280 PRINT "ENTER THE LOAD IMPEDANCE(>0)"
00290 INPUT R1
00300 IF R1 > 0 THEN 00320
00310 GOTO 00280
00320 REM GET CUTOFF FREQUENCY IN HERTZ
00330 PRINT "ENTER FREQUENCY AT CUTOFF(3 DB DOWN)"
00340 INPUT F0
00350 IF F0 > 0 THEN 00380
00360 PRINT "FREQUENCY MUST BE POSITIVE"
00370 GOTO 00330
00380 REM GET THE SLOPE FREQUENCY
00390 PRINT "ENTER SLOPE FREQUENCY"
00400 INPUT F1
00410 REM CHECK FREQUENCY RANGE
00420 IF F1>F0 THEN 00450
00430 PRINT "SLOPE FREQUENCY IS INCORRECT"
00440 GOTO 00390
00450 REM GET THE SLOPE ATTENUATION IN DB
00460 PRINT "ENTER THE ATTENUATION DESIRED AT ";F1
00470 INPUT A
00480 REM CHECK THAT ATTENUATION IS VALID
00490 IF A>0 THEN 00530
00500 PRINT "ATTENUATION MUST BE >0"
00510 GOTO 00460
00520 REM GET THE RIPPLE FACTOR IN DB
00530 PRINT "ENTER THE MAXIMUM ALLOWED RIPPLE"
00540 INPUT D
00550 REM CHECK THE RIPPLE GIVEN
00560 IF D>0 THEN 00610
00570 PRINT "RIPPLE MUST BE GREATER THAN 0"
00580 GOTO 00530
00590 REM ALL THE VALUES HAVE BEEN OBTAINED
00600 REM FROM THE USER - SO WE CAN
00610 REM BEGIN THE CALCULATION PROCESS
00620 REM FIRST WE CALCULATE THE RIPPLE
00630 REM AS A FUNCTIONAL VALUE EPSILON
00640 Q=10^(D/10)
00650 E=SQR(Q/10)
00660 REM CALCULATE THE PARAMETER ALPHA
00670 A1=4/(E*E)
00680 A1=A1*(10^(A/10)-1)-2
```

```
00690 REM CALCULATE THE PARAMETER BETA
00700 REM FIRST NORMALIZE THE FREQUENCIES
00710 W0=F0*6.283185307
00720 W1=F1*6.283185307
00730 REM CONVERT TO STANDARDIZED FORM
00740 W=W1/W0
00750 REM CONTINUE BETA CALCULATION
00760 B=SQR(W*W-1)
00770 B=W+B
00780 REM CALCULATE FIRST ESTIMATE OF N
00790 REM WHERE N IS THE NUMBER OF SHUNT
00800 REM AND SERIES GROUPS COMBINED
00810 N=LOG(A1)/LOG(B)
00820 REM WE NOW LOOP THRU THE VALUES OF N
00830 REM USING THE NEWTON METHOD FOR
00840 REM FINDING THE ROOT OF AN EQUATION
00850 REM ADJUSTING FOR THE BEST VALUE OF N
00860 REM CALCULATE THE INCREMENTAL VALUE
00870 REM USING THE EXISTING N
00880 V3=B^N
00890 V8=V3+(1/V3)-A1
00900 V4=V3-(1/V3)
00910 V5=V8/V4
00920 V7=LOG(B)*2
00930 V6=V5/V7
00940 REM ADJUST N TO THE NEW VALUE
00950 REM USING THE CORRECTION
00960 REM JUST CALCULATED (V6)
00970 N=N-V6
00980 REM IS THE CORRECTION VALUE TOO
00990 REM TO WORRY FURTHER ABOUT
01000 IF ABS(V6)<.00001 THEN 01040
01010 GOTO 00880
01020 REM ROUND UP THE VALUE TO
01030 REM THE NEXT INTEGER
01040 N=INT(N+1)
01050 REM CALCULATE THE CONSTANT GAMMA
01060 Y1=D/40
01070 Y2=Y1*LOG(10)*2
01080 Y3=EXP(Y2)
01090 Y4=(Y3-1)/(Y3+1)
01100 Y5=Y4^(1/(2*N))
01110 Y6=Y4-(1/Y4)
01120 Y-(Y6*Y6)
01130 REM CALCULATE BASIC CONVERSIONS
01140 REM SHUNT CONVERSIONS
01150 REM SIN COMPONENT ADJUSTMENT
01160 N1=3.141592654/(2*N)
01170 REM COMPONENT ADJUST FOR SIN
01180 N6=2*N1
01190 REM CALCULATE THE INITIAL VALUES
01200 REM STARTING WITH A(V1)
01210 V1=SIN(N1)
01220 REM THE FIRST G VALUE (G1)
01230 G1=2*V1/(SQR(Y))
01240 REM THE FIRST B VALUE
01250 B1=SIN(N6)
01260 B1=B1*B1+Y
01270 REM BEGIN PRINTOUT RUN
01280 PRINT TAB(5);"*******************************"
01290 PRINT "*"
```

```
01300 PRINT TAB(10);"DESIGN RESULTS FOR A"
01310 PRINT TAB(16); "CHEBYSHEV"
01320 PRINT TAB(16);"LOW-PASS"
01330 PRINT TAB(17);"FILTER"
01340 PRINT "*"
01350 PRINT TAB(5);"******************************"
01360 PRINT "*"
01370 PRINT "CUTOFF FREQUENCY(HZ)",FO
01380 PRINT "ATTENUATION SLOPE FREQUENCY",F1
01390 PRINT "ATTENUATION SLOPE VALUE(DB)",A
01400 PRINT "        AS A VOLTAGE RATIO",10^(A/20)
01410 PRINT "RIPPLE OR CUTOFF PRE-RISE(DB)",D
01420 PRINT "RIPPLE AS A VOLTAGE RATIO",10^(D/20)
01430 PRINT "LOAD/SOURCE IMPEDANCE",R1
01440 PRINT "CALCULATED FILTER ORDER",INT((N+1)/2)
01450 PRINT "*"
01460 PRINT TAB(10);"*******************"
01470 PRINT "*"
01480 PRINT TAB(10);"COMPONENT VALUES"
01490 PRINT "*"
01500 PRINT TAB(10);"*******************"
01510 PRINT "*"
01520 PRINT "STAGE","COMPONENT","VALUE","TYPE"
01530 PRINT "------------------------------------------
01540 PRINT "*"
01550 REM PRESET THE VALUES FOR THE FIRST PASS
01560 G2=G1
01570 V2=V1
01580 B2=B1
01590 REM RESULT-PRINT LOOP
01600 FOR I = 1 TO N
01610 REM IS THIS THE FIRST PASS
01620 IF I = 1 THEN 01650
01630 REM CALCULATE G2 FOR THIS PASS
01640 G2=4*V1/(B1*G1)
01650 V1=SIN((2*I-1)*N1)
01660 B1=SIN(I*N6)
01670 B1=B1*B1+Y
01680 REM IS THIS AN ODD OR EVEN PASS
01690 IF INT((I+.01)/2)*2=I THEN 01750
01700 REM ODD PASS - DO SHUNT
01710 M1=G2/(R1*WO)
01720 PRINT I,"CAPACITOR",M1,"SHUNT"
01730 GOTO 01770
01740 REM EVEN PASS - DO SERIES
01750 M1=G2*R1/WO
01760 PRINT I,"INDUCTOR",M1,"SERIES"
01770 G1=G2
01780 NEXT I
01790 PRINT "*"
01800 PRINT "*"
01810 PRINT "********* END OF RUN *********"
01820 STOP
01830 END
```

COLOR CODE FOR RESISTORS

This program converts color code to ohmic value, and the reverse. It assumes that all entries are integers. The ohmic color code is:

COLOR	VALUE
Black	0
Brown	1
Red	2
Orange	3
Yellow	4
Green	5
Blue	6
Violet	7
Gray	8
White	9

Color Code For Resistors

EXAMPLE

```
RUN
DO YOU WISH TO CONVERT TO OHMIC VALUE
OR TO COLOR CODE
ENTER 1 FOR OHMIC VALUE
2 FOR COLOR CODE
? 1
ENTER COLOR CODE, SEPARATE EACH COLOR
WITH A COMMA.
IF THERE IS NO TOLERANCE BAND,
ENTER 'NONE'
? BROWN, BLACK, BROWN, GOLD
10 5% TOLERANCE
RUN COMPLETE
RUN
DO YOU WISH TO CONVERT TO OHMIC VALUE
OR TO COLOR CODE
ENTER 1 FOR OHMIC VALUE
2 FOR COLOR CODE.
? 2
ENTER DESIRED VALUE
? 10
RESISTOR COLOR CODE FOR 10
BROWN BLACK BROWN, 20% TOLERANCE
RUN COMPLETE
```

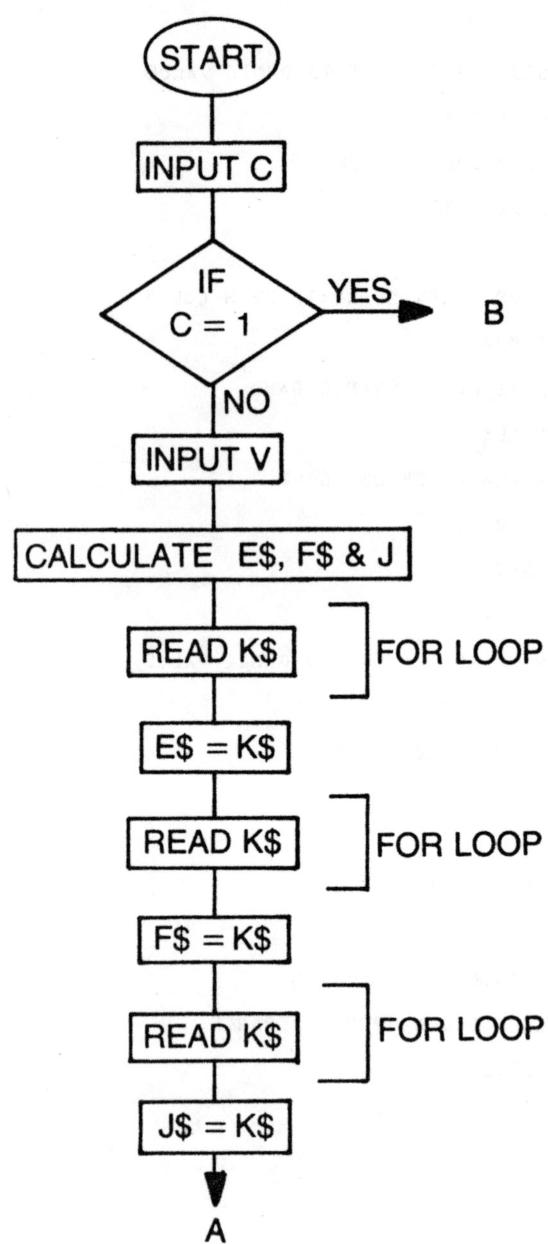

Color Code For Resistors

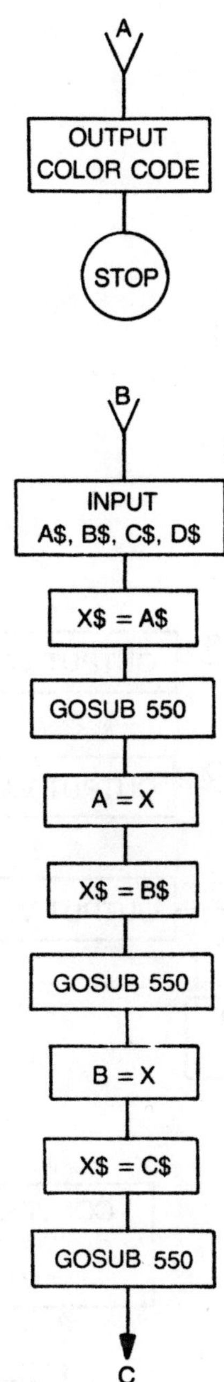

Color Code For Resistors

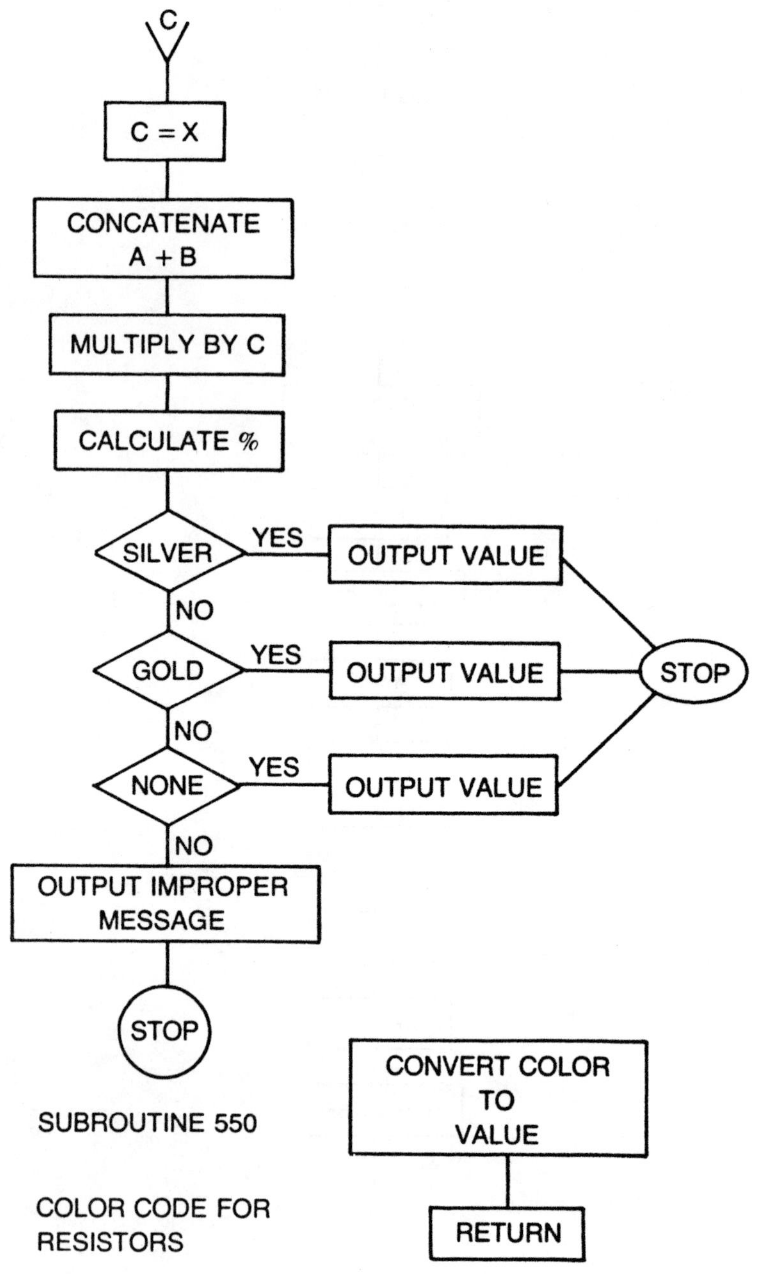

SUBROUTINE 550

COLOR CODE FOR
RESISTORS

PROGRAM

```
00010  REM THIS PROGRAM CONVERTERS
       RESISTOR
00020  REM COLOR CODES INTO VALUES AND
00030  REM THE REVERSE
00040  REM KT 1978
00050  PRINT ''DO YOU WISH TO CONVERT
       TO OHMIC VALUE''
00060  PRINT ''OR TO COLOR CODE''
00070  PRINT ''ENTER 1 FOR OHMIC VALUE''
00080  PRINT ''2 FOR COLOR CODE.''
00090  INPUT C
00100  IF C = 1 THEN 00390
00110  PRINT
00120  PRINT ''ENTER DESIRED VALUE''
00130  INPUT V
00140  V = INT{ABS{V}}
00150  V$ = STR${V}
00160  L = LEN V$
00170  E$ = SUBSTR {V$,1,1}
00180  F$ = SUBSTR{V$,2,1}
00190  I = L - 2
00200  RESTORE
00210  FOR I = 1 TO VAL{E$} H
00220  READ K$
00230  NEXT I
00240  E$ = K$
00250  RESTORE
00260  FOR I = 1 TO VAL{F$} + 1
00270  READ K$
00280  NEXT I
```

```
00290  F$ = K$
00300  RESTORE
00310  FOR I = 1 TO J + 1
00320  READ K$
00330  NEXT I
00340  J$ = K$
00350  PRINT
00360  PRINT ''RESISTOR COLOR CODE FOR
       ''; V
00370  PRINT E$;'' '';F$;'' '';J$;''
       ''; ''20% TOLERANCE''
00380  STOP
00390  PRINT
00400  PRINT ''ENTER COLOR CODE,
       SEPARATE EACH COLOR''
00410  PRINT ''WITH A COMMA''
00420  PRINT ''IF THERE IS NO
       TOLERANCE BAND,''
00430  PRINT ''ENTER 'NONE'.''
00440  INPUT A$, B$, C$, D$.
00450  X$ = A$
00460  GOSUB 550
00470  A = X
00480  X$ = B$
00490  GOSUB 550
00500  B = X
00510  X$ = C$
00520  GOSUB 550
00530  C = X
00540  GOTO 870
```

```
00550 IF X$ = ''BLACK'' THEN 670
00560 IF X$ = ''BROWN'' THEN 690
00570 IF X$ = ''RED'' THEN 710
00580 IF X$ = ''ORANGE'' THEN 730
00590 IF X$ = ''YELLOW'' THEN 750
00600 IF X$ = ''GREEN'' THEN 770
00610 IF X$ = ''BLUE'' THEN 790
00620 IF X$ = ''VIOLET'' THEN 810
00630 IF X$ = ''GRAY'' THEN 830
00640 IF X$ = ''WHITE'' THEN 850
00650 PRINT ''IMPROPER ENTRY''
00660 STOP
00670 X = 0
00680 GOTO 860
00690 X = 1
00700 GOTO 860
00710 X = 2
00720 GOTO 860
00730 X = 3
00740 GOTO 860
00750 X = 4
00760 GOTO 860
00770 X = 5
00780 GOTO 860
00790 X = 6
00800 GOTO 860
00810 X = 7
00820 GOTO 860
00830 X = 8
00840 GOTO 860
```

```
00850  X = 9
00860  RETURN
00870  J$ = STR${A}
00880  K$ = STR${B}
00890  J$ = J$ + K$
00900  J = VAL {J$}
00910  J = J*10 C
00920  IF D$ = ''SILVER'' THEN 970
00930  IF D$ = ''GOLD'' THEN 990
00940  IF D$ = ''NONE'' THEN
00950  PRINT ''IMPROPER ENTRY''
00960  STOP
00970  PRINT J ''10% TOLERANCE''
00980  STOP
00990  PRINT J ''5% TOLERANCE''
01000  STOP
01010  PRINT J ''20% TOLERANCE''
01020  STOP
01030  DATA BLACK, BROWN, RED,
       ORANGE, YELLOW
01040  DATA GREEN, BLUE, VIOLET,
       GRAY, WHITE
01050  END
```

CROSS CORRELATION FOR CURVES

This program does a cross correlation between two given curves through use of the least-squares method. It returns the degree of similarity between two sets of data. Only one data item is required at a time (for each curve), as it is assumed that the independent variable is the same for each pair, representing the two dependent variables for the two curves.

```
EXAMPLE

  ENTER THE NUMBER OF DATA POINTS TO BE ENTERED
  ? 9
  ENTER THE DATA AS PAIRS OF NUMBERS
  ENTER X AND Y ? 1,1
  ENTER X AND Y ? 2,2
  ENTER X AND Y ? 3,3
  ENTER X AND Y ? 4,4
  ENTER X AND Y ? 5,5
  ENTER X AND Y ? 6,6
  ENTER X AND Y ? 22,22
  ENTER X AND Y ? 33,33
  ENTER X AND Y ? 431,431
  THE CORRELATION COEFFICIENT FOR  9
  DATA PAIRS IS  1
RUN

 78/03/09. 19.56.05.
PROGRAM   CROSSCR

ENTER THE NUMBER OF DATA POINTS TO BE ENTERED
? 5
```

```
ENTER THE DATA AS PAIRS OF NUMBERS
ENTER X AND Y ? 1,3
ENTER X AND Y ? 2,5
ENTER X AND Y ? 3,7
ENTER X AND Y ? 7,9
ENTER X AND Y ? 9,134
THE CORRELATION COEFFICIENT FOR  5
DATA PAIRS IS  .772154
```

```
PROGRAM   CROSSCR

ENTER THE NUMBER OF DATA POINTS TO BE ENTERED
? 7

ENTER THE DATA AS PAIRS OF NUMBERS
ENTER X AND Y ? 304,70
ENTER X AND Y ? 60,10
ENTER X AND Y ? 30,81
ENTER X AND Y ? 231,70
ENTER X AND Y ? 78,10
ENTER X AND Y ? 64,3
ENTER X AND Y ? 30,4678
THE CORRELATION COEFFICIENT FOR  7
DATA PAIRS IS -.331803
```

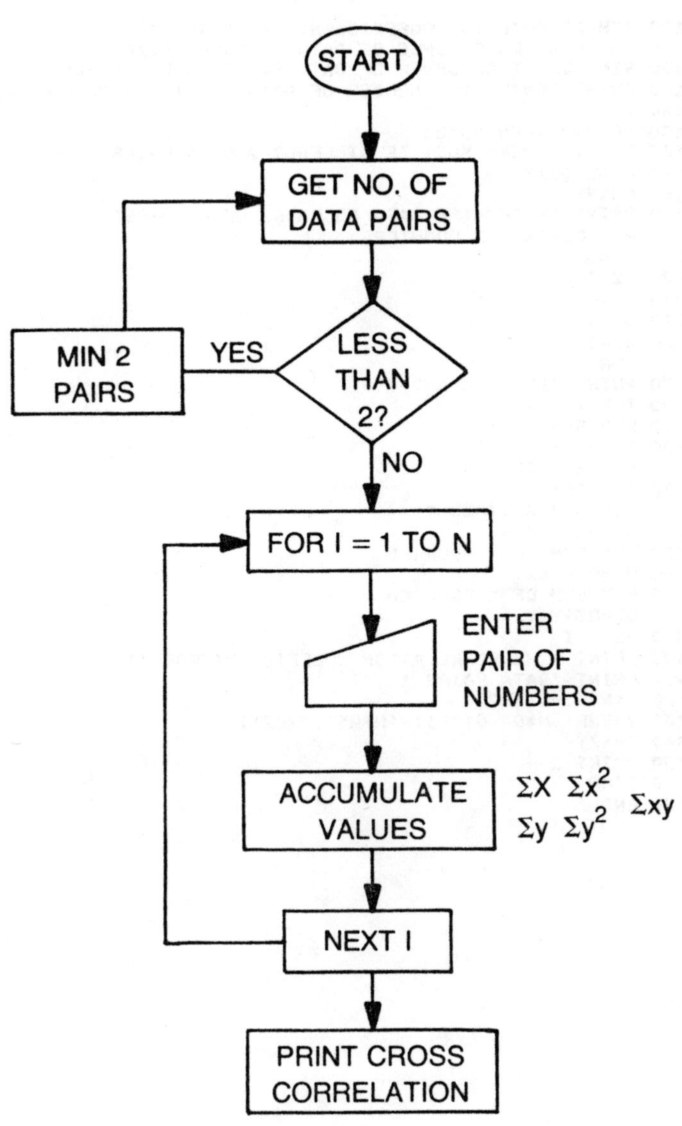

Cross Correlation for Curves

PROGRAM

```
00100 REM COMPUTE THE COEFFICIENT OF CORRELATION
00110 REM FOR TWO STRINGS OF DATA OF EQUAL SIZE
00120 REM  GET THE NUMBER OF DATA PAIRS TO BE ENTERED
00130 PRINT 'ENTER THE NUMBER OF DATA POINTS TO BE ENTERED'
00140 INPUT N
00150 IF N>2 THEN 00180
00160 PRINT 'THERE MUST BE AT LEAST 2 DATA PAIRS'
00170 GOTO 00130
00180 PRINT
00190 PRINT 'ENTER THE DATA AS PAIRS OF NUMBERS'
00200 REM CLEAR THE COUNTERS
00210 Q1=0
00220 Q2=0
00230 Q3=0
00240 Q4=0
00250 Q5=0
00260 FOR I = 1 TO N
00270 PRINT 'ENTER X AND Y';
00280 INPUT X,Y
00290 REM SUM OF X
00300 Q1=Q1+X
00310 REM SUM OF Y'S
00320 Q2=Q2+Y
00330 REM SUM X TIMES Y
00340 Q3=Q3+X*Y
00350 REM SUM OF X SQUARED
00360 Q4=Q4+X*X
00370 REM SUM OF Y SQUARED
00380 Q5=Q5+Y*Y
00390 NEXT I
00400 PRINT 'THE CORRELATION COEFFICIENT FOR ';N
00410 PRINT 'DATA PAIRS IS ';
00420 X=N*Q3-Q1*Q2
00430 Y=SQR((N*Q4-Q1*Q1)*(N*Q5-Q2*Q2))
00440 Z=X/Y
00450 PRINT Z
00460 STOP
00470 END
```

GREATEST COMMON DENOMINATOR

This routine calculates the greatest common denominator between any two numbers. This program uses the Euclidean algorithm to solve for the GCD, which is the largest number that will divide evenly into both given numbers. The Euclidean algorithm follows:

```
 Input x,y
 x = absolute x
 y = absolute y
┌→find x−y (INTEGER OF x/y)
│ is the above 0
│ if yes, then y is the GCD
│ if no continue
│ x=y
│ y = x−y (integer of x/y)
└←return to find x−y(integer of x/y)
```

EXAMPLE

```
**********GREATEST COMMON DENOMINATOR**********

ENTER ANY TWO NUMBERS
ENTER 0,0 TO STOP EXECUTION
? 5,6
THE GCD IS  1


ENTER ANY TWO NUMBERS
ENTER 0,0 TO STOP EXECUTION
? 34,89
THE GCD IS  1


ENTER ANY TWO NUMBERS
ENTER 0,0 TO STOP EXECUTION
? 50,250
THE GCD IS  50

ENTER ANY TWO NUMBERS
ENTER 0,0 TO STOP EXECUTION
? 12,144
THE GCD IS  12


ENTER ANY TWO NUMBERS
ENTER 0,0 TO STOP EXECUTION
? 500,250
THE GCD IS  250


ENTER ANY TWO NUMBERS
ENTER 0,0 TO STOP EXECUTION
? 678,234
THE GCD IS  6


ENTER ANY TWO NUMBERS
ENTER 0,0 TO STOP EXECUTION
? 4567,8973
THE GCD IS  1


ENTER ANY TWO NUMBERS
ENTER 0,0 TO STOP EXECUTION
? 0,0
```

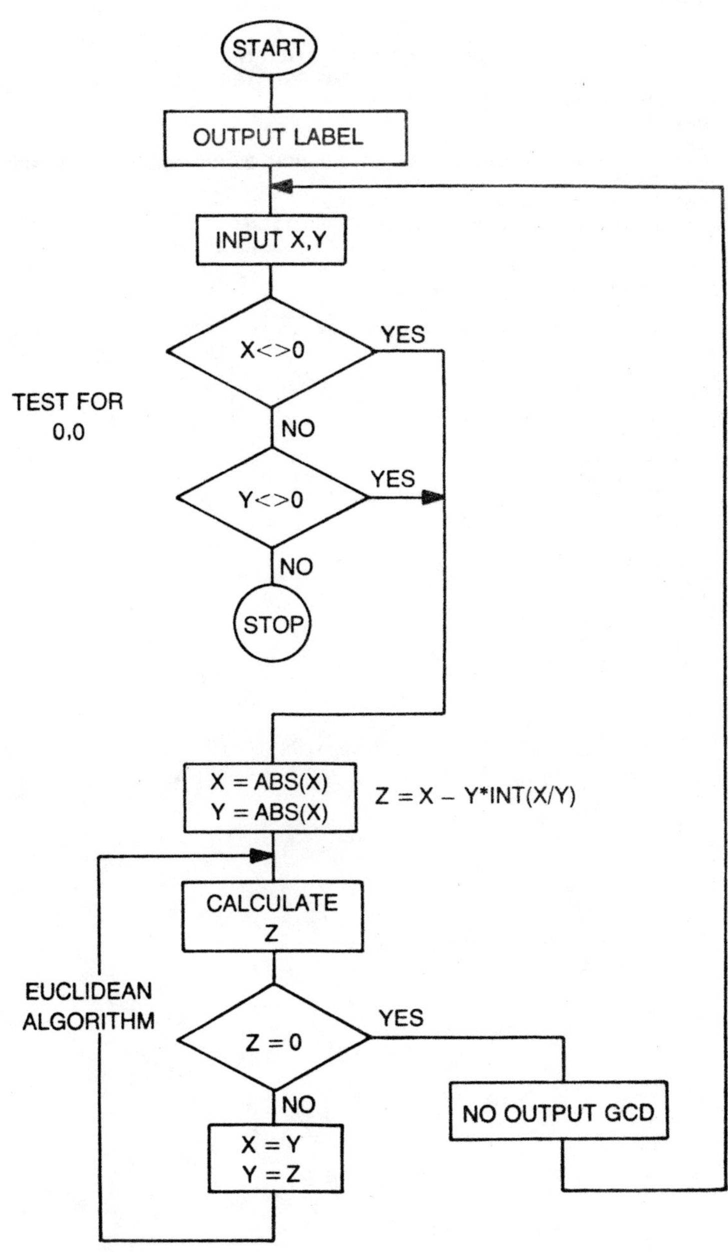

Greatest Common Denominator

PROGRAM

```
00005 REM THIS PROGRAM COMPUTES USING THE
00010 REM EUCLIDEAN ALGORITHM THE GREATEST
00015 REM COMMON DENOMINATOR
00020 REM KT 3/3/78
00025 PRINT
00030 PRINT"**********GREATEST COMMON DENOMINATOR**********"
00035 PRINT
00040 PRINT"ENTER ANY TWO NUMBERS"
00045 PRINT"ENTER 0,0 TO STOP EXECUTION"
00050 INPUT X,Y
00055 IF X<>0 THEN 00075
00060 IF Y<>0 THEN 00075
00065 STOP
00070 REM USE EUCLIDEAN ALGORITHM
00075 X=ABS(X)
00080 Y=ABS(Y)
00085 Z=X-Y*INT(X/Y)
00090 IF Z=0 THEN 00115
00095 X=Y
00100 Y=Z
00105 GOTO 00085
00110 REM NOW WE OUTPUT WHAT WE FOUND
00115 PRINT"THE GCD IS ";Y
00120 PRINT
00125 GOTO 00035
00130 END
```

HARMONIC CURVE FITTING

This program performs a Fourier analysis on a set of input points representing a set of cyclic curves. Since any curve may be derived from a group of sinusoidal curves, and since these sine-wave curves represent actual harmonics, this program is very useful for electronic designers working with frequency synthesizers, spectrum analyzers, real-time harmonic generators and analyzers, and so forth.

This program produces the harmonic magnitudes and phase angles required to generate the curve specified by the input. It further calculates the number of harmonics which will fit the input model. This is called harmonic curve fitting.

EXAMPLE

```
PROGRAM   HARMONY

INPUT NUMBER OF DATA POINTS AND NUMBER OF HARMONICS
? 8,5
INPUT DATA POINT  1 ? -1
INPUT DATA POINT  2 ? -1
INPUT DATA POINT  3 ? -1
INPUT DATA POINT  4 ? -1
INPUT DATA POINT  5 ? 1
INPUT DATA POINT  6 ? 1
INPUT DATA POINT  7 ? 1
INPUT DATA POINT  8 ? 1

 K            COMP(K)          PHASE(K)         DEVIATION

 0            -.142857          ----             1.14286
 1             1.28399          192.857          .571429
 2             .317119         -64.2857          .45825
 3             .45825           218.571          7.09805E-9
 4             .45825          -38.5714          .45825
 5             .317119          244.286          .571429

 K            INPUT(K)         BEST(K) (FOR     3              HARMONICS)

 1            -1               -1.
 2            -1               -1.
 3            -1               -1.
 4            -1               -1.
 5             1                1.
 6             1                1.
 7             1                1.
 8             1               -1.


PROGRAM   HARMONY

INPUT NUMBER OF DATA POINTS AND NUMBER OF HARMONICS
? 12,99
DO NOT EXCEED THE NUMBER OF POINTS ALLOWED(50)
INPUT NUMBER OF DATA POINTS AND NUMBER OF HARMONICS
? 1,7
A MINIMUM OF 3 POINTS/HARMONICS ARE REQUIRED
INPUT NUMBER OF DATA POINTS AND NUMBER OF HARMONICS
? 12,7
INPUT DATA POINT  1 ? 0
INPUT DATA POINT  2 ? 10
INPUT DATA POINT  3 ? 9
INPUT DATA POINT  4 ? 8
INPUT DATA POINT  5 ? 7
INPUT DATA POINT  6 ? 6
INPUT DATA POINT  7 ? 5
INPUT DATA POINT  8 ? 4
INPUT DATA POINT  9 ? 3
INPUT DATA POINT  10  ? 2
INPUT DATA POINT  11  ? 1
INPUT DATA POINT  12  ? 0

 K            COMP(K)          PHASE(K)         DEVIATION

 0             5.               ----             5.
 1             3.54947         -16.3636          4.
 2             1.84966         -32.7273          3.
 3             1.32319         -49.0909          2.
 4             1.09935         -65.4545          1.
 5             1.01028         -81.8182          3.60723E-8
 6             1.01028          261.818          1
 7             1.09935          245.455          2.
```

```
K             INPUT(K)        BEST(K) (FOR    5      HARMONICS)

1             0               -2.06057E-13
2             10               10.
3             9                9.
4             8                8.
5             7                7.
6             6                6.
7             5                5.
8             4                4.
9             3                3.
10            2                2.
11            1                1.
12            0               -8.37364E-8

PROGRAM   HARMONY

INPUT NUMBER OF DATA POINTS AND NUMBER OF HARMONICS
? 9,3
INPUT DATA POINT  1 ? 0
INPUT DATA POINT  2 ? 0
INPUT DATA POINT  3 ? 0
INPUT DATA POINT  4 ? 0
INPUT DATA POINT  5 ? 1
INPUT DATA POINT  6 ? 1
INPUT DATA POINT  7 ? 1
INPUT DATA POINT  8 ? 1
INPUT DATA POINT  9 ? 0
```

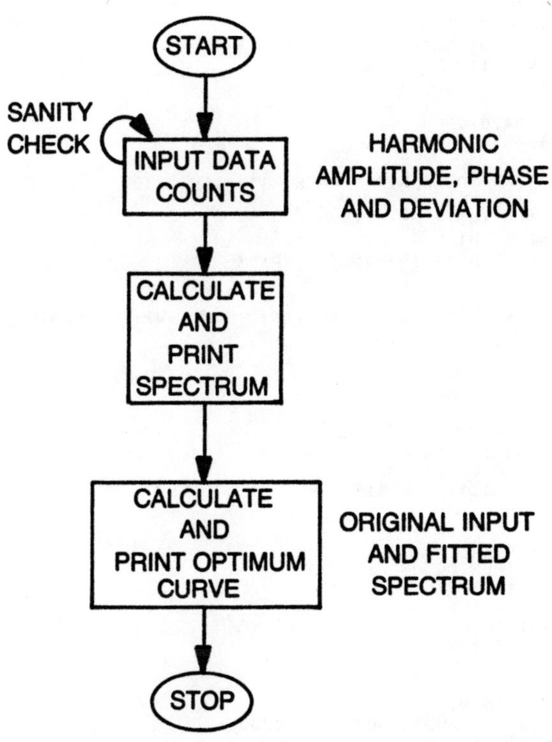

Harmonic Curve Fitting

K	COMP(K)	PHASE(K)	DEVIATION
0	.5	----	.5
1	.653281	202.5	.25
2	1.26918E-9	-45.0001	.25
3	.270598	247.5	3.28183E-9

K	INPUT(K)	BEST(K) (FOR	3	HARMONICS)
1	0	-3.28183E-9		
2	0	2.32062E-9		
3	0	-1.26916E-9		
4	0	-1.79489E-9		
5	1	1.		
6	1	1.		
7	1	1.		
8	1	1.		
9	0	3.28185E-9		

PROGRAM

```
00100 DIM V1(50),V2(50),V3(50),V4(50),V5(50)
00110 P1=3.14159265
00120 PRINT 'INPUT NUMBER OF DATA POINTS AND NUMBER OF HARMONICS'
00130 INPUT W1,H1
00140 IF W1<51 AND H1<51 THEN 00170
00150 PRINT 'DO NOT EXCEED THE NUMBER OF POINTS ALLOWED(50)'
00160 GOTO 00120
00170 IF W1>2 AND H1>2 THEN 00200
00180 PRINT 'A MINIMUM OF 3 POINTS/HARMONICS ARE REQUIRED'
00190 GOTO 00120
00200 FOR I1=1 TO W1
00210 PRINT 'INPUT DATA POINT ';I1;
00220 INPUT V1(I1)
00230 NEXT I1
00240 W1=W1-1
00250 GOSUB 00470
00260 W1=W1+1
00270 PRINT
00280 PRINT ' K','COMP(K)','PHASE(K)','DEVIATION'
00290 PRINT
00300 PRINT ' 0',W5,' ----',W8
00310 FOR K=1 TO H1
00320 PRINT K,V4(K),V3(K)*180/P1,V5(K)
00330 NEXT K
00340 PRINT
00350 PRINT ' K','INPUT(K)','BEST(K) (FOR ',W2,'HARMONICS)'
00360 PRINT
00370 Y=-W6
00380 FOR I1=1 TO W1
00390 Y=Y+W6
00400 V2(I1)=W5
00410 FOR K=1 TO W2
00420 V2(I1)=V2(I1)+V4(K)*SIN(K*Y+V3(K))
00430 NEXT K
00440 PRINT I1,V1(I1),V2(I1)
00450 NEXT I1
00460 STOP
00470 W6=2*P1/W1
00480 IF H1>0 THEN 00500
00490 H1=INT(W1/2)+1
00500 W5=0
00510 FOR I1=1 TO W1
00520 W5=W5+V1(I1)/W1
00530 NEXT I1
00540 W8=0
00550 FOR I1=1 TO W1
00560 IF ABS(V1(I1)-W5)<=W8 THEN 00580
00570 W8=ABS(V1(I1)-W5)
00580 NEXT I1
00590 FOR K=1 TO H1
```

```
00600 W7=0
00610 W4=0
00620 Y=-W6
00630 FOR I1=1 TO W1
00640 Y=Y+W6
00650 W7=W7+(1/P1)*V1(I1)*SIN(K*Y)*W6
00660 W4=W4+(1/P1)*V1(I1)*COS(K*Y)*W6
00670 NEXT I1
00680 IF K<>W1/2 THEN 00710
00690 W7=W7/2.
00700 W4=W4/2.
00710 V4(K)=SQR(W7^2+W4^2)
00720 W3=W4/W7
00730 IF W7<>0 THEN 00760
00740 IF W4>0 THEN 00760
00750 W3=-W3
00760 V3(K)=ATN(W3)
00770 IF W7>=0 THEN 00790
00780 V3(K)=V3(K)+P1
00790 Y=-W6
00800 V5(K)=0
00810 FOR I1=1 TO W1
00820 Y=Y+W6
00830 IF K<>1 THEN 00850
00840 V2(I1)=W5
00850 V2(I1)=V2(I1)+V4(K)*SIN(K*Y+V3(K))
00860 IF ABS(V1(I1)-V2(I1))<=V5(K) THEN 00880
00870 V5(K)=ABS(V1(I1)-V2(I1))
00880 NEXT I1
00890 IF K<>1 THEN 00920
00900 M1=V5(1)
00910 W2=1
00920 IF V5(K)>=M1 THEN 00950
00930 M1=V5(K)
00940 W2=K
00950 NEXT K
00960 RETURN
00970 END
```

HEX/DECIMAL CONVERSIONS

The hex program allows the user to convert from hexadecimal to decimal (base 16 to base 10) and from decimal to hex. To signify that a number is hex, type an H before the hexadecimal number (see the test run).

EXAMPLE

```
THIS PROGRAM CONVERTS HEXADECIMAL NUMBERS
TO  DECIMAL AND ALSO DOES THE REVERSE
IF A HEX NUMBER IS ENTERED PRECEED IT WITH
A H

ENTER A NUMBER? 32
DECIMAL 32 IS 0020 HEXADECIMAL

ENTER A NUMBER? H2345
HEX H2345 IS  9029  DECIMAL

ENTER A NUMBER? 9029
DECIMAL 9029 IS 2345 HEXADECIMAL

ENTER A NUMBER? H1943
HEX H1943 IS  6467  DECIMAL

ENTER A NUMBER? HFFFE
HEX HFFFE IS  65534  DECIMAL
```

```
ENTER A NUMBER? 6789
DECIMAL 6789 IS 1A85 HEXADECIMAL

ENTER A NUMBER? 1949
DECIMAL 1949 IS 079D HEXADECIMAL

ENTER A NUMBER? 34
DECIMAL 34 IS 0022 HEXADECIMAL

ENTER A NUMBER? H654D
HEX H654D IS  25932  DECIMAL

ENTER A NUMBER? END
RUN COMPLETE.
```

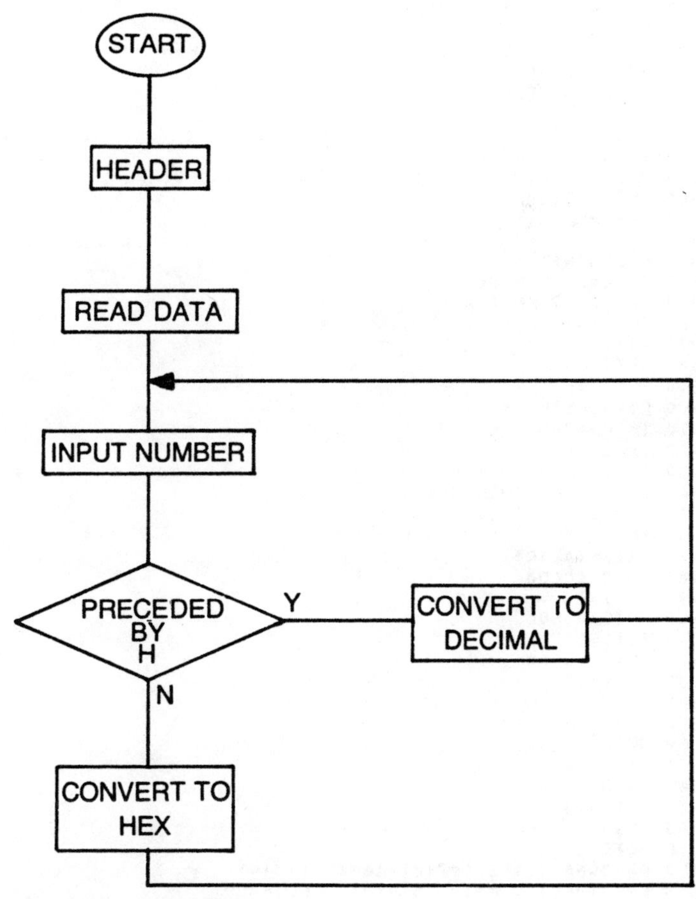

Hex/Decimal Conversions

PROGRAM

```
00010 REM THIS PROGRAM CONVERTS HEX TO DECIMAL
00020 REM KT APRIL 1978
00030 PRINT
00040 PRINT"THIS PROGRAM CONVERTS HEXADECIMAL NUMBERS TO"
00050 PRINT"DECIMAL AND ALSO DOES THE REVERSE"
00060 PRINT"IF A HEX NUMBER IS ENTERED PRECEED IT WITH A H"
00070 PRINT
00080 DATA 4096,256,16,1
00090 H$="0123456789ABCDEF"
00100 RESTORE
00110 PRINT
00120 PRINT"ENTER A NUMBER";
00130 INPUT N$
00140 IF SUBSTR(N$,1,1)="H" THEN 00310
00150 IF N$="END" THEN 00650
00160 N=VAL(N$)
00170 X$=""
00180 J=4
00190 READ P
00200 FOR I=1 TO 16
00210 IF N-I*P<0 THEN 00250
00220 NEXT I
00230 PRINT"YOU GOOFED, WE FOUND AN INPUT ERROR"
00240 GOTO 00100
00250 X$=X$+SUBSTR(H$,I,1)
00260 N=N-(I-1)*P
00270 J=J-1
00280 IF J>0 THEN 00190
00290 PRINT"DECIMAL ";N$;" IS ";X$;" HEXADECIMAL"
00300 GOTO 00100
00310 REM HEX
00320 J=2
00330 L=LEN(N$)
00340 IF L<2 THEN 00230
00350 IF L>5 THEN 00230
00360 FOR I=1 TO 4
00370 Z(I)=0
00380 NEXT I
00390 FOR I=6-L TO 4
00400 Q$=SUBSTR(N$,J,1)
00410 IF Q$="A" THEN 00490
00420 IF Q$="B" THEN 00510
00430 IF Q$="C" THEN 00530
00440 IF Q$="D" THEN 00550
00450 IF Q$="E" THEN 00570
00460 IF Q$="F" THEN 00590
00470 Z(I)=VAL(Q$)
00480 GOTO 00600
00490 Z(I)=10
00500 GOTO 00600
00510 Z(I)=11
00520 GOTO 00600
00530 Z(I)=12
00540 GOTO 00600
00550 Z(I)=12
00560 GOTO 00600
00570 Z(I)=14
00580 GOTO 00600
00590 Z(I)=15
00600 J=J+1
00610 NEXT I
00620 D=4096*Z(1)+256*Z(2)+16*Z(3)+Z(4)
00630 PRINT"HEX ";N$;" IS ";D;" DECIMAL"
00640 GOTO 00100
00650 END
```

LISSAJOUS SIMULATION

This program simulates an oscilloscope representation of Lissajous patterns.

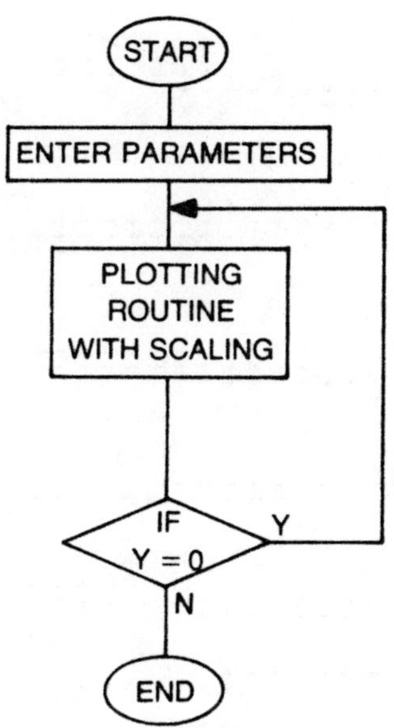

Lissajous Simulation

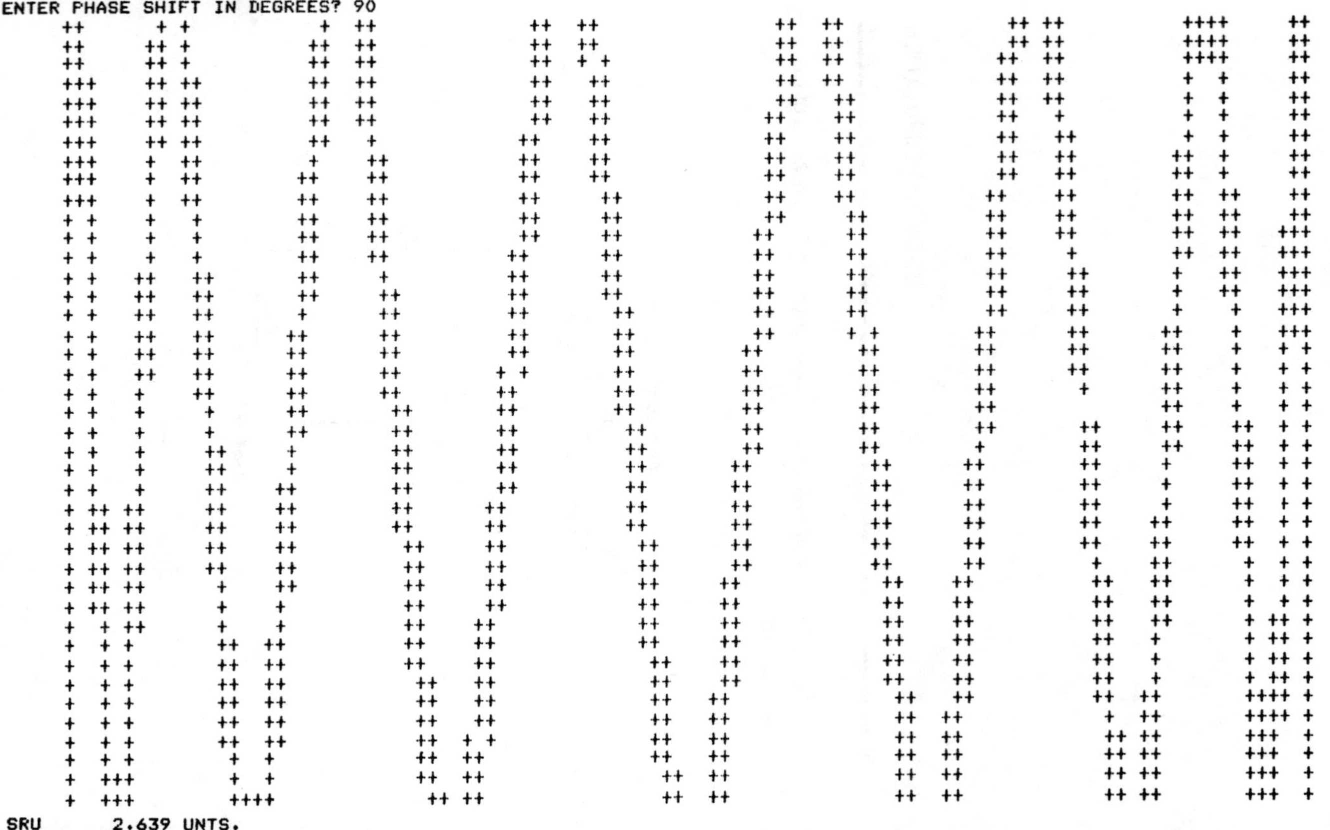
ENTER THE TWO FREQUENCIES ? 1,16
ENTER PHASE SHIFT IN DEGREES? 90
SRU 2.639 UNTS.

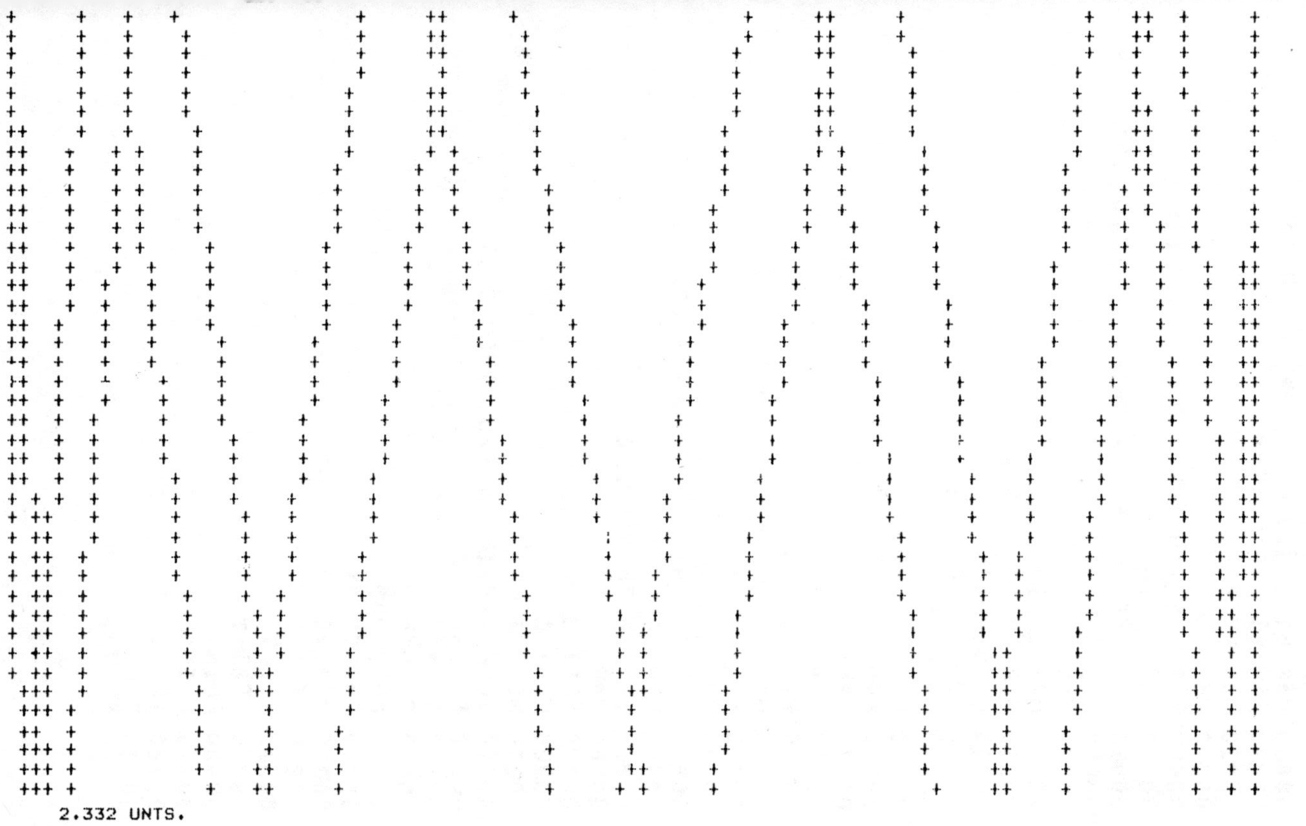

SRU 2.332 UNTS.

RUN COMPLETE.

PROGRAM

```
00010 REM LISSAJOUS PATTERN GENERATOR
00020 REM KT APRIL 1978
00030 DIM M(120)
00040 PRINT
00050 PRINT"ENTER THE TWO FREQUENCIES";
00060 INPUT A,B
00070 PRINT"ENTER PHASE SHIFT IN DEGREES";
00080 INPUT P
00090 T=0
00100 MARGIN 133
00110 REM MAIN PROGRAM
00120 GOTO 00400
00130 FOR Y=-20 TO 20
00140 F=-Y/20
00150 H=0
00160 K=0
00170 K=K+1
00180 FOR X=0 TO 1
00190 P1=3.14159
00200 N=(X*(P1-2*F)+F+2*P1*K)*A/B+(57.296*P)
00210 FOR C=-.5 TO .5
00220 FOR J=0 TO T*A/B
00230 R=INT(SIN(N+J*C)*160/3+200/3)
00240 M(R)=1
00250 IF R<H THEN 00270
00260 H=R
00270 NEXT J
00280 NEXT C
00290 NEXT X
00300 IF K*A/B>INT(K*A/B) THEN 00170
00310 FOR X=1 TO H
00320 IF M(X)=1 THEN 00350
00330 PRINT" ";
00340 GOTO 00370
00350 PRINT"+";
00360 M(X)=0
00370 NEXT X
00380 PRINT
00390 NEXT Y
00400 PRINT
00410 PRINT
00420 IF Y=0 THEN 00130
00430 END
```

MOVING AVERAGE

This program generates a moving average up to 150 points The averaging bucket size may also be up to 150 points.

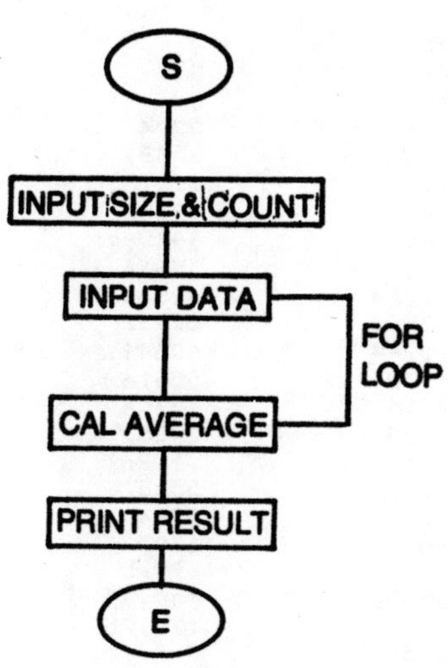

EXAMPLE

```
ENTER MOVING AVERAGE SLOT SIZE
? 7
ENTER THE OBSERVATION COUNT
? 1
OBSERVATION COUNT MUST BE BETWEEN 2 AND 150
ENTER THE OBSERVATION COUNT
? 25

ENTER THE DATA POINTS

? 22
? 44
? 88
? 176
? 352
? 704
? 1408
? 2816
? 5632
? 11264
? 22528
? 11264
? 5632
? 2816
? 1408
? 704
? 352
? 176
? 88
? 44
? 22
? 11
? 5.5
? 2.75
? 5.5
```

SLOT	SINGLE VALUE	ACCUMED VALUE	MOVING AVERAGE
1	22	0	0
2	44	0	0
3	88	0	0
4	176	2794	399.143
5	352	5588	798.286
6	704	11176	1596.57
7	1408	22352	3193.14
8	2816	44704	6386.29
9	5632	55616	7945.14
10	11264	60544	8649.14
11	22528	61952	8850.29
12	11264	60544	8649.14
13	5632	55616	7945.14
14	2816	44704	6386.29
15	1408	22352	3193.14
16	704	11176	1596.57
17	352	5588	798.286
18	176	2794	399.143
19	88	1397	199.571
20	44	698.5	99.7857
21	22	349.25	49.8929
22	11	178.75	25.5357
23	5.5	0	0
24	2.75	0	0
25	5.5	0	0

```
00100 REM CALCULATE ANY MOVING AVERAGE
00110 REM AND TOTAL OF TO 150
00120 REM THE SIZE OF THE MOVING AVERAGE
00130 REM SLOT IS SET FIRST (S)
00140 REM COUNT OF INPUT DATA POINTS
00150 REM IS GIVEN NEXT
00160 DIM V1(150),V2(150),V3(150)
00170 PRINT 'ENTER MOVING AVERAGE SLOT SIZE'
00180 INPUT S
00190 S=INT(S)
00200 IF S>150 OR S<2 THEN 00220
00210 GOTO 00240
00220 PRINT 'SLOT SIZE MUST BE BETWEEN 2 AND 150'
00230 GOTO 00170
00240 PRINT 'ENTER THE OBSERVATION COUNT'
00250 INPUT N
00260 N=INT(N)
00270 IF N>2 AND N<=150 THEN 00300
00280 PRINT 'OBSERVATION COUNT MUST BE BETWEEN 2 AND 150'
00290 GOTO 00240
00300 PRINT
00310 PRINT 'ENTER THE DATA POINTS'
00320 PRINT
00330 FOR I1=1 TO N
00340 INPUT V3(I1)
00350 NEXT I1
00360 Q2=INT(.5*S+1)
00370 Q1=Q2-S+N
00380 W4=0
00390 FOR I1=Q2 TO Q1
00400 W4=W4+1
00410 I3=W4+S-1
00420 FOR I2=W4 TO I3
00430 V2(I1)=V2(I1)+V3(I2)
00440 NEXT I2
00450 NEXT I1
00460 FOR I1=Q2 TO Q1
00470 V1(I1)=V2(I1)/S
00480 NEXT I1
00490 PRINT
00500 PRINT 'SLOT','SINGLE VALUE','ACCUMED VALUE','MOVING AVERAGE'
00510 PRINT
00520 FOR I1=1 TO N
00530 PRINT I1,V3(I1),V2(I1),V1(I1)
00540 NEXT I1
00550 END
```

MEAN, STANDARD DEVIATION AND VARIANCE OF GROUPED OR UNGROUPED DATA

This program computes the arithmetic mean, the standard deviation, and the variance of grouped or ungrouped data. It also allows the user to input the entire population, or only a sample of the population.

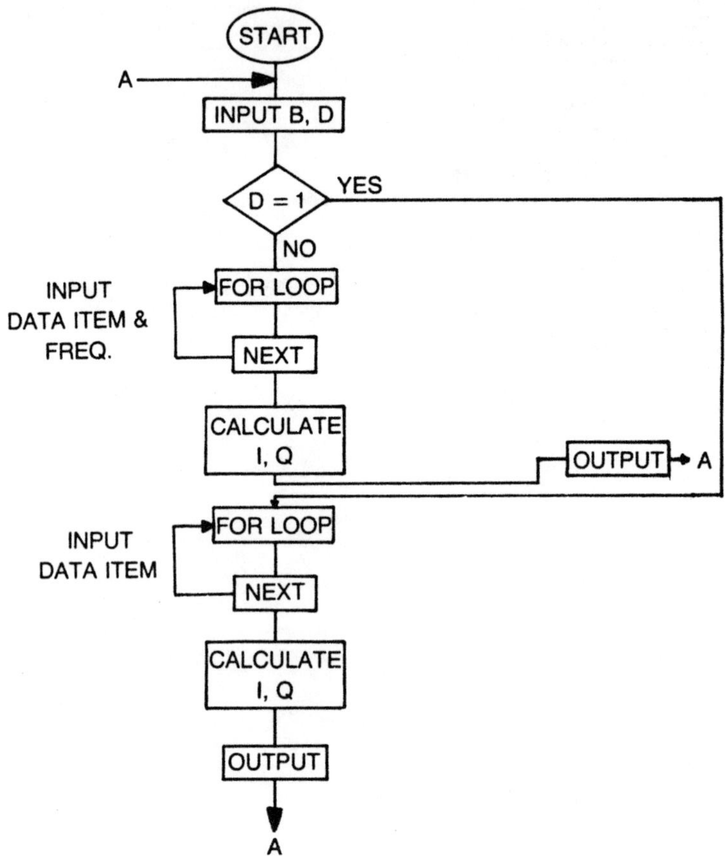

Mean, Standard Deviation and Variance of Grouped or Ungrouped Data

EXAMPLE

```
**ARITHMETIC MEAN-STANDARD DEVIATION-VARIANCE**

DATA IS POPULATION (0) OR A SAMPLE (1)
? 0

DATA IS UNGROUPED (1) OR GROUPED (0)
? 0

ENTER THE NUMBER OF OBSERVATIONS

? 5
DATA ITEM, FREQ ? 1,9
DATA ITEM, FREQ ? 4,8
DATA ITEM, FREQ ? 5,7
DATA ITEM, FREQ ? 4,8
DATA ITEM, FREQ ? 3,9

MEAN               SD                 VARIANCE
 3.29268            1.36585            1.86556

TYPE 1 TO CONTINUE, 0 TO STOP
? 1

DATA IS POPULATION (0) OR A SAMPLE (1)
? 1

DATA IS UNGROUPED (1) OR GROUPED (0)
? 0

ENTER THE NUMBER OF OBSERVATIONS

? 5
DATA ITEM, FREQ ? 1,9
DATA ITEM, FREQ ? 4,8
DATA ITEM, FREQ ? 5,7
DATA ITEM, FREQ ? 4,8
DATA ITEM, FREQ ? 3,9

MEAN               SD                 VARIANCE
 3.29268            1.38282            1.9122

TYPE 1 TO CONTINUE, 0 TO STOP
? 1

DATA IS POPULATION (0) OR A SAMPLE (1)
? 0

DATA IS UNGROUPED (1) OR GROUPED (0)
? 1
```

```
ENTER THE NUMBER OF OBSERVATIONS

? 5
DATA ITEM ? 1
DATA ITEM ? 4
DATA ITEM ? 5
DATA ITEM ? 4

DATA ITEM ? 3

MEAN              SD               VARIANCE
 3.4               1.35647          1.84

TYPE 1 TO CONTINUE, 0 TO STOP
? 1

DATA IS POPULATION (0) OR A SAMPLE (1)
? 1

DATA IS UNGROUPED (1) OR GROUPED (0)
? 1

ENTER THE NUMBER OF OBSERVATIONS

? 5
DATA ITEM ? 1
DATA ITEM ? 4
DATA ITEM ? 5
DATA ITEM ? 4
DATA ITEM ? 3

MEAN              SD               VARIANCE
 3.4               1.51658          2.3

TYPE 1 TO CONTINUE, 0 TO STOP
? 0
```

```
PROGRAM
LIST

 78/03/12. 13.12.27.
PROGRAM   MSDV

00005 REM THIS PROGRAM COMPUTES THE MEAN, THE VARIANCE
00010 REM AND THE STANDARD DEVIATION FOR
00015 REM GROUPED AND UNGROUPED DATA. IT ALSO ALLOWS DATA
00020 REM TO BE EITHER THE POPULATION OR A SAMPLE
00025 REM KT 12/3/78
00030 PRINT
00035 PRINT"**ARITHMETIC MEAN-STANDARD DEVIATION-VARIANCE**"
00040 PRINT
00045 PRINT"DATA IS POPULATION (0) OR A SAMPLE (1)"
00050 INPUT B
00055 PRINT
00060 PRINT"DATA IS UNGROUPED (1) OR GROUPED (0)"
00065 INPUT D
00070 PRINT
00075 PRINT"ENTER THE NUMBER OF OBSERVATIONS"
00080 PRINT
00085 INPUT A
00090 I=0
00095 N=0
00100 M=0
00105 IF D=1 THEN 00160
00110 FOR J=1 TO A
00115 PRINT"DATA ITEM, FREQ";
00120 INPUT C,D
00125 I=I+D*C
00130 M=M+D
00135 N=N+D*C^2
00140 NEXT J
00145 I=I/M
00150 Q=(N-M*I^2)/(M-B)
00155 GOTO 00200
00160 FOR J=1 TO A
00165 PRINT"DATA ITEM";
00170 INPUT K
00175 M=M+K
00180 N=N+K^2
00185 NEXT J
00190 I=M/A
00195 Q=(N-A*I^2)/(A-B)
00200 PRINT
00205 PRINT"MEAN","SD","VARIANCE"
00210 PRINT I,SQR(Q),Q
00215 PRINT
00220 PRINT"TYPE 1 TO CONTINUE, 0 TO STOP"
00225 INPUT C
00230 IF C=1 THEN 00040
00235 END
```

OP AMP DESIGN

This routine designs an operational amplifier circuit using as information the minimum desired frequency in hertz, the desired close-loop gain and response with actual closed-loop gain (taking into account closed-loop errors), loop gain, error, true output impedance, transient response in seconds, the offset output voltage, linearity (THD), and the two resistors required.

The circuit uses the popular 301A integrated circuit. The program supplies a standard EIA value for R2 and the required resistance for R1. For best results, use a trimming resistor to achieve as close as possible a value for R1, as this bias resistor is quite critical.

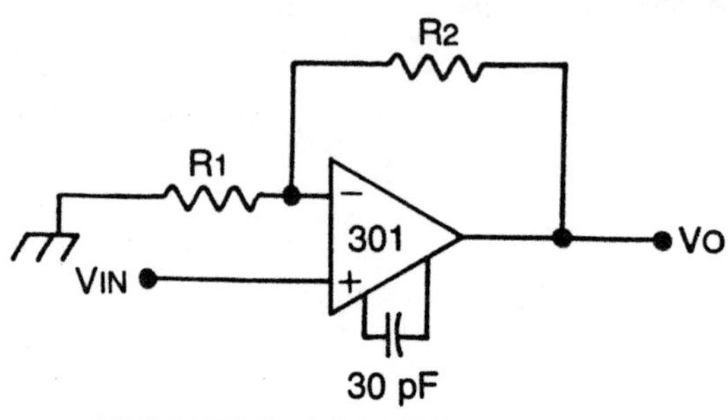

FREQUENCY COMPENSATING

EXAMPLE

PROGRAM OPAMP

```
**********OPERATIONAL AMPLIFIER OPTIMIZATION**********
                      USING THE
                        301A



ENTER DESIRED MINIMUM FREQUENCY RESPONSE IN HZ
? 4567

ENTER DESIRED CLOSED LOOP GAIN
? 2345
REDUCE EITHER FREQUENCY RESPONSE OR GAIN
SO THAT THE PRODUCT OF THE TWO
WILL BE LESS THAN OR EQUAL TO 1E06
ENTER DESIRED MINIMUM FREQUENCY RESPONSE IN HZ
? 345

ENTER DESIRED CLOSED LOOP GAIN
? 1000

ACTUAL CLOSED LOOP GAIN IS  743.494

LOOP GAIN IS  2.89855

ERROR CAUSED BY CLOSED LOOP
CONFIGURATION IS  25.6506 %

OUTPUT IMPEDANCE IS  38.4758

TRANSIENT RESPONSE IS  1.01449E-3

OFFSET OUTPUT VOLTAGE IS  2

LINEARITY (THD) IS  .256506 %

FEEDBACK RESISTOR R2 IS  100000

FEEDBACK/BIAS RESISTOR R1 IS  100

**********OPERATIONAL AMPLIFIER OPTIMIZATION**********
                      USING THE
                        301A



ENTER DESIRED MINIMUM FREQUENCY RESPONSE IN HZ
? 300

ENTER DESIRED CLOSED LOOP GAIN
? 23

ACTUAL CLOSED LOOP GAIN IS  22.8424

LOOP GAIN IS  144.928

ERROR CAUSED BY CLOSED LOOP
CONFIGURATION IS  .685272 %
```

```
OUTPUT IMPEDANCE IS  1.02791

TRANSIENT RESPONSE IS  1.16667E-3

OFFSET OUTPUT VOLTAGE IS  .046

LINEARITY (THD) IS  6.85272E-3 %

FEEDBACK RESISTOR R2 IS  2200

FEEDBACK/BIAS RESISTOR R1 IS  100

**********OPERATIONAL AMPLIFIER OPTIMIZATION**********
                         USING THE
                           301A


ENTER DESIRED MINIMUM FREQUENCY RESPONSE IN HZ
? 23

ENTER DESIRED CLOSED LOOP GAIN
? 1256

ACTUAL CLOSED LOOP GAIN IS  1220.74

LOOP GAIN IS  34.6164

ERROR CAUSED BY CLOSED LOOP
CONFIGURATION IS  2.80769 %

OUTPUT IMPEDANCE IS  4.21154

TRANSIENT RESPONSE IS  1.52174E-2

OFFSET OUTPUT VOLTAGE IS  2.512

LINEARITY (THD) IS  2.80769E-2 %

FEEDBACK RESISTOR R2 IS  150000

FEEDBACK/BIAS RESISTOR R1 IS  119
```

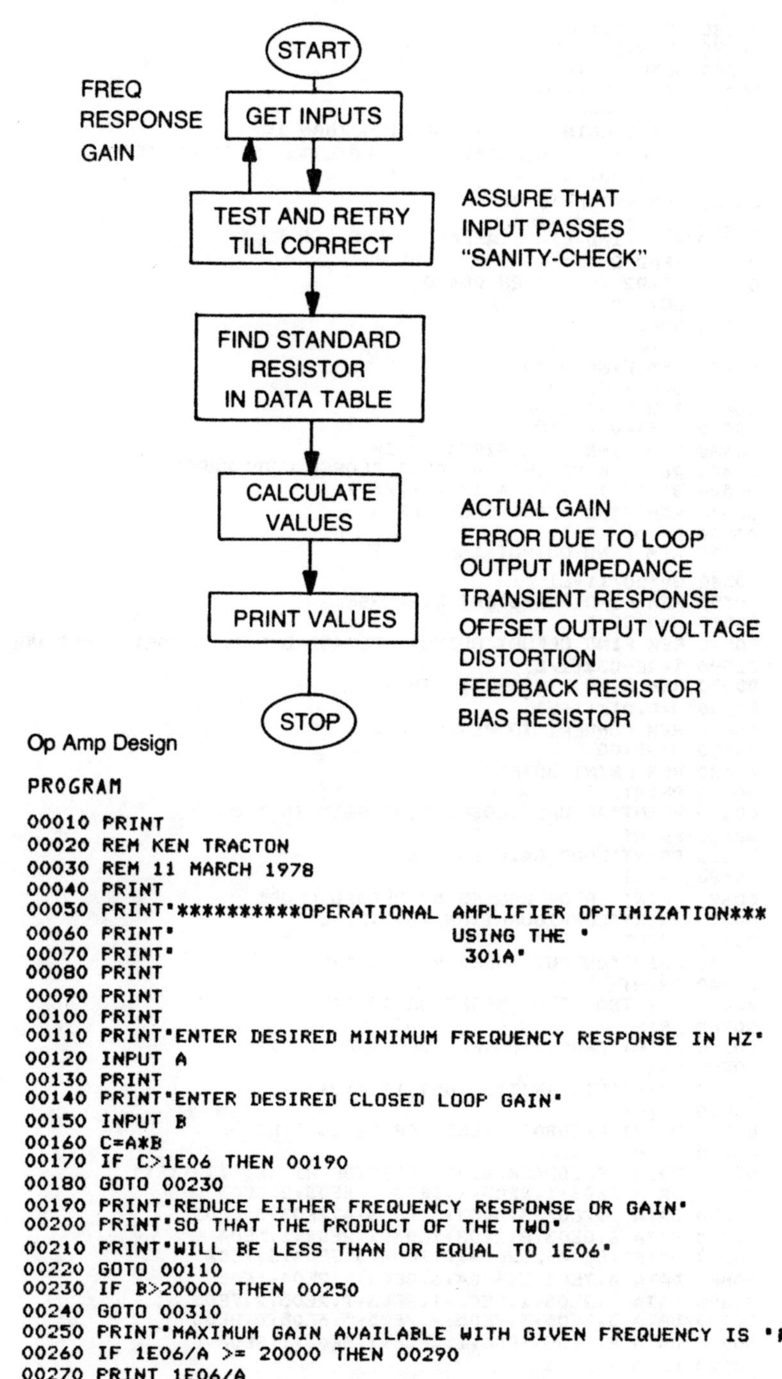

Op Amp Design

PROGRAM

```
00010 PRINT
00020 REM KEN TRACTON
00030 REM 11 MARCH 1978
00040 PRINT
00050 PRINT"**********OPERATIONAL AMPLIFIER OPTIMIZATION***
00060 PRINT"                                USING THE "
00070 PRINT"                                 301A"
00080 PRINT
00090 PRINT
00100 PRINT
00110 PRINT"ENTER DESIRED MINIMUM FREQUENCY RESPONSE IN HZ"
00120 INPUT A
00130 PRINT
00140 PRINT"ENTER DESIRED CLOSED LOOP GAIN"
00150 INPUT B
00160 C=A*B
00170 IF C>1E06 THEN 00190
00180 GOTO 00230
00190 PRINT"REDUCE EITHER FREQUENCY RESPONSE OR GAIN"
00200 PRINT"SO THAT THE PRODUCT OF THE TWO"
00210 PRINT"WILL BE LESS THAN OR EQUAL TO 1E06"
00220 GOTO 00110
00230 IF B>20000 THEN 00250
00240 GOTO 00310
00250 PRINT"MAXIMUM GAIN AVAILABLE WITH GIVEN FREQUENCY IS ";
00260 IF 1E06/A >= 20000 THEN 00290
00270 PRINT 1E06/A
```

```
00280 GOTO 00110
00290 PRINT"20000"
00300 GOTO 00110
00310 IF B<10 THEN 00330
00320 GOTO 00360
00330 PRINT"GAIN MUST BE GREATER THAN 10"
00340 PRINT"IF LINEARITY AND STABILITY IS TO EXIST"
00350 GOTO 00110
00360 REM ESTIMATE R2
00370 R2=(100*B)-100
00380 REM FIND EIA STANDARD VALUE FOR R2
00390 READ C
00400 IF R2 <= C THEN 00420
00410 GOTO Q0390
00420 R2=C
00430 R1=R2/(B-1)
00440 REM FIND BETA
00450 D=R1/(R1+R2)
00460 REM FIND LOOP GAIN
00470 E=(1E06/A)*D
00480 REM FIND TRUE SIGNAL GAIN
00490 REM TAKING INTO ACCOUNT CLOSED LOOP ERRORS
00500 B=((R1+R2)/R1)*(1/(1+(1/E)))
00510 REM FIND PERCENTAGE ERROR
00520 F=100/(E+1)
00530 REM FIND OUTPUT IMPEDANCE
00540 G=150/(1+E)
00550 REM FIND TRANSIENT RESPONSE
00560 H=0.35/A
00570 REM FIND OFFSET OUTPUT VOLTAGE DUE TO OFFSET INPUT VOLTAGE
00580 I=2E-03*(1/D)
00590 REM FIND LINEARITY (THD)
00600 J=0.01/(1+E)
00610 REM CONVERT TO PERCENTAGE
00620 J=J*100
00630 REM PRINT OUTPUT
00640 PRINT
00650 PRINT"ACTUAL CLOSED LOOP GAIN IS ";B
00660 PRINT
00670 PRINT"LOOP GAIN IS ";E
00680 PRINT
00690 PRINT"ERROR CAUSED BY CLOSED LOOP"
00710 PRINT"CONFIGURATION IS ";F;"%"
00720 PRINT
00730 PRINT"OUTPUT IMPEDANCE IS ";G
00740 PRINT
750 PRINT"TRANSIENT RESPONSE IS ";H
00760 PRINT
00770 PRINT"OFFSET OUTPUT VOLTAGE IS ";I
00780 PRINT
00790 PRINT"LINEARITY (THD) IS ";J;"%"
00800 PRINT
00810 PRINT"FEEDBACK RESISTOR R2 IS ";R2
00820 PRINT
00830 PRINT"FEEDBACK/BIAS RESISTOR R1 IS ";INT(R1)
00840 DATA 1E03,1.2E03,1.5E03,1.8E03,2.2E03
00850 DATA 2.7E03,3.3E03,3.9E03,4.7E03,5.6E03
00860 DATA 6.8E03,8.2E03,1E04,1.2E04,1.5E04
00870 DATA1.8E04,2.2E04,2.7E04,3.3E04,3.9E04
00880 DATA 4.7E04,5.6E04,6.8E04,8.2E04,1E05
00890 DATA 1.2E05,1.5E05,1.8E05,2.2E05,2.7E05
00900 DATA 3.3E05,3.9E05,4.7E05,5.6E05,6.8E05
00910 DATA 8.2E05,1E06,1.2E06,1.5E06,1.8E06
00920 DATA 2.2E06
00930 END
```

POLYGON AREA

This program computes the area of any polygon with no more than 30 vertices. You must enter the x,y coordinates (Cartesian) for each vertex, $V_1 \ldots V_{30}$. There is no need to enter the last vertex, as it is the same as the first one. (In the diagram shown, the program will automatically connect V_7 to V_1 to close the program.)

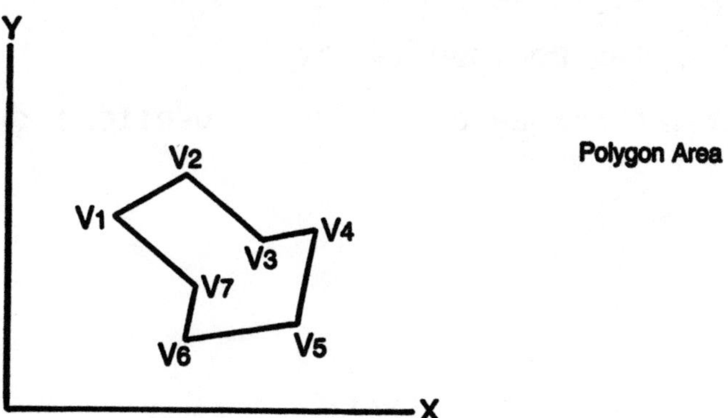

Area = $(x_1+x_2)(y_1-y_2) + (x_2 + x_3)(y_2-y_3) \ldots (x_n+x_1)(y_n-y_1)$
where
n = number of vertices
x,y = Cartesian coordinates

EXAMPLE

```
+++++++++AREA OF A POLYGON+++++++++

ENTER THE NUMBER OF VERTICES (VERTICES <=30)
ENTER 0 TO STOP
? 4

COORDINATES

VERTEX  1   ? 0,0
VERTEX  2   ? 0,1
VERTEX  3   ? 1,1
VERTEX  4   ? 1,0

AREA OF THE POLYGON IS  1

ENTER THE NUMBER OF VERTICES (VERTICES <=30)
ENTER 0 TO STOP
? 5

COORDINATES

VERTEX  1   ? 1,2
VERTEX  2   ? 2,6
VERTEX  3   ? 6,8
VERTEX  4   ? 1,1
VERTEX  5   ? 0,0

AREA OF THE POLYGON IS  10

ENTER THE NUMBER OF VERTICES (VERTICES <=30)
ENTER 0 TO STOP
```

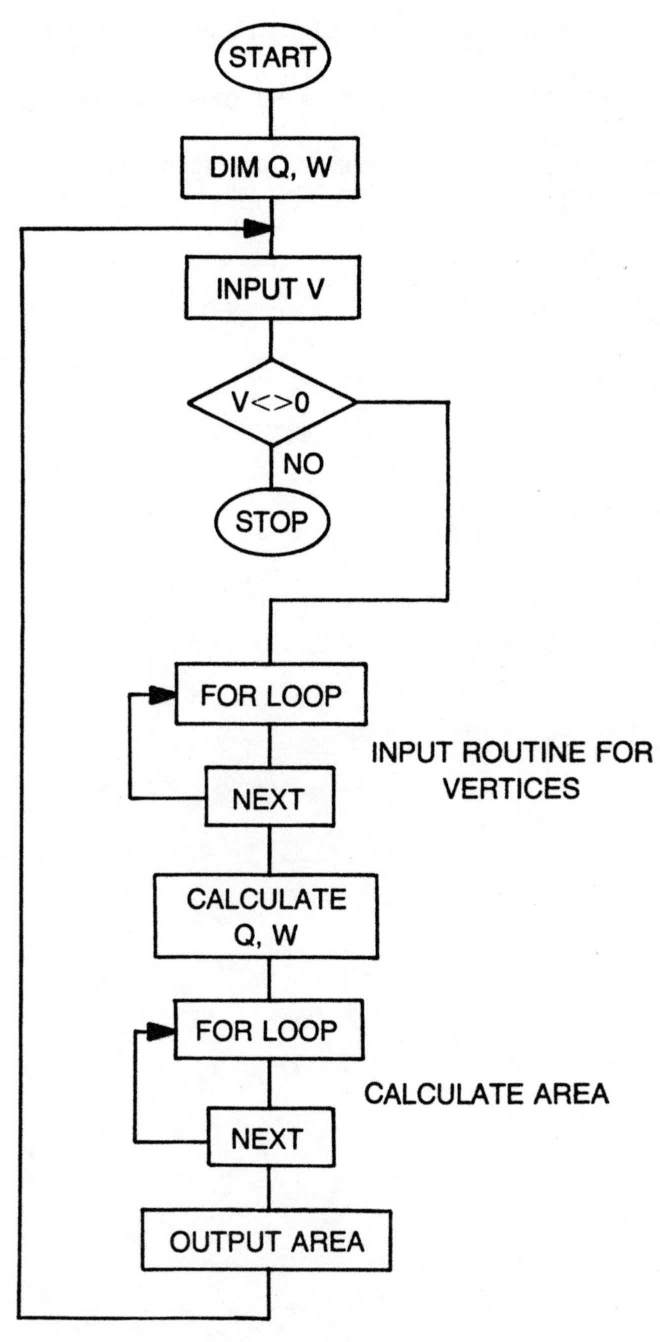
START
DIM Q, W
INPUT V
V<>0
NO
STOP
FOR LOOP
INPUT ROUTINE FOR VERTICES
NEXT
CALCULATE Q, W
FOR LOOP
CALCULATE AREA
NEXT
OUTPUT AREA

PROGRAM

```
00005 REM THIS PROGRAM COMPUTES THE AREA OF A POLYGON
00010 REM KT 8/3/78
00015 PRINT
00020 PRINT"+++++++++AREA OF A POLYGON+++++++++"
00025 PRINT
00030 DIM Q(31),W(31)
00035 PRINT"ENTER THE NUMBER OF VERTICES (VERTICES <=30)"
00040 PRINT"ENTER 0 TO STOP"
00045 INPUT V
00050 IF V<>0 THEN 00060
00055 STOP
00060 PRINT
00065 PRINT"COORDINATES"
00070 PRINT
00075 FOR J=1 TO V
00080 PRINT"VERTEX ";J;" ";
00085 INPUT Q(J),W(J)
00090 NEXT J
00095 Q(V+1)=Q(1)
00100 W(V+1)=W(1)
00105 Z=0
00110 FOR J=1 TO V
00115 Z=Z+(Q(J)+Q(J+1))*(W(J)-W(J+1))
00120 NEXT J
00125 PRINT
00130 PRINT"AREA OF THE POLYGON IS ";Z/2
00135 PRINT
00140 GOTO 00035
00145 END
```

PRIME FACTOR

This routine takes as its input any number and outputs the prime factor in power form. This program is unique in that it will accept both positive and negative numbers.

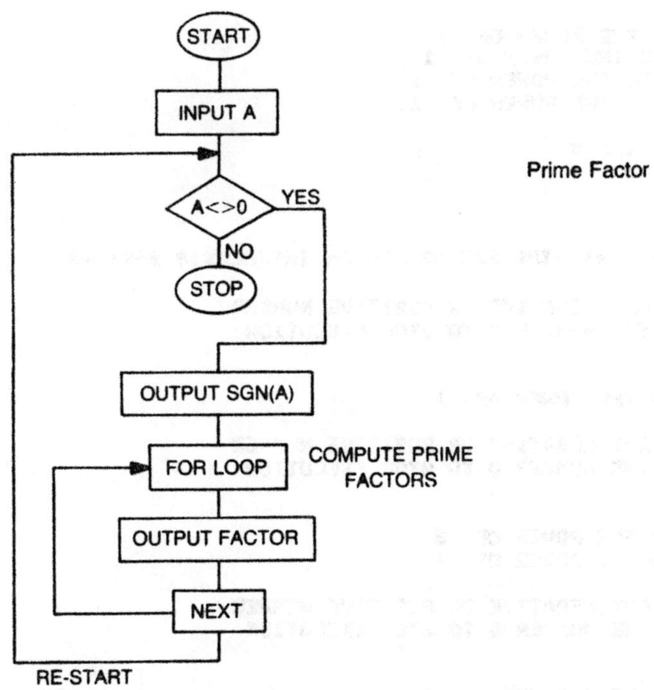

Prime Factor

EXAMPLE

```
*+*+*+*+*+*PRIME FACTORS OF AN INTEGER*+*+*+*+*+*

ENTER ANY NEGATIVE OR POSITIVE NUMBER
ENTER THE NUMBER 0 TO STOP EXECUTION
? 123
 1
 3  TO THE POWER OF  1
 41  TO THE POWER OF  1

ENTER ANY NEGATIVE OR POSITIVE NUMBER
ENTER THE NUMBER 0 TO STOP EXECUTION
? 5000
 1
 2  TO THE POWER OF  3
 5  TO THE POWER OF  4

ENTER ANY NEGATIVE OR POSITIVE NUMBER
ENTER THE NUMBER 0 TO STOP EXECUTION
? 125688
 1
 2  TO THE POWER OF  3
 3  TO THE POWER OF  1
 5237  TO THE POWER OF  1

ENTER ANY NEGATIVE OR POSITIVE NUMBER
ENTER THE NUMBER 0 TO STOP EXECUTION
? 14444498
 1
 2  TO THE POWER OF  1
 59  TO THE POWER OF  1
 167  TO THE POWER OF  1
 733  TO THE POWER OF  1

*TIME LIMIT*


*+*+*+*+*+*PRIME FACTORS OF AN INTEGER*+*+*+*+*+*

ENTER ANY NEGATIVE OR POSITIVE NUMBER
ENTER THE NUMBER 0 TO STOP EXECUTION
? 2
 1
 2  TO THE POWER OF  1

ENTER ANY NEGATIVE OR POSITIVE NUMBER
ENTER THE NUMBER 0 TO STOP EXECUTION
? 56
 1
 2  TO THE POWER OF  3
 7  TO THE POWER OF  1

ENTER ANY NEGATIVE OR POSITIVE NUMBER
ENTER THE NUMBER 0 TO STOP EXECUTION
? 121
 1
 11  TO THE POWER OF  2
```

```
ENTER ANY NEGATIVE OR POSITIVE NUMBER
ENTER THE NUMBER 0 TO STOP EXECUTION
? 101
 1
 101  TO THE POWER OF  1

ENTER ANY NEGATIVE OR POSITIVE NUMBER
ENTER THE NUMBER 0 TO STOP EXECUTION
? 3000
 1
 2  TO THE POWER OF  3
 3  TO THE POWER OF  1
 5  TO THE POWER OF  3

ENTER ANY NEGATIVE OR POSITIVE NUMBER
ENTER THE NUMBER 0 TO STOP EXECUTION
? 45321
 1
 3  TO THE POWER OF  1
 15107  TO THE POWER OF  1

ENTER ANY NEGATIVE OR POSITIVE NUMBER
ENTER THE NUMBER 0 TO STOP EXECUTION
? 0
```

PROGRAM

```
00005 REM THIS PROGRAM FINDS THE PRIME
00010 REM FACTORS OF AN INTEGER
00015 REM KT 5/2/78
00020 PRINT
00025 PRINT"*+*+*+*+*+*PRIME FACTORS OF AN INTEGER*+*+*+*+*+*"
00030 PRINT
00035 PRINT
00040 PRINT
00045 PRINT
00050 REM ACCEPT INPUT
00055 PRINT"ENTER ANY NEGATIVE OR POSITIVE NUMBER"
00060 PRINT"ENTER THE NUMBER 0 TO STOP EXECUTION"
00065 INPUT A
00070 REM VERIFY THAT EXECUTION IS WANTED
00075 IF A<>0 THEN 00090
00080 STOP
00085 REM THE NUMBER 1 OR -1 IS ALWAYS A FACTOR
00090 PRINT SGN (A)
00095 A=ABS(A)
00100 REM COMPUTE FACTORS
00105 FOR J=2 TO A
00110 K=0
00115 IF A/J <> INT(A/J) THEN 00135
00120 A=A/J
00125 K=K+1
00130 GOTO 00115
00135 IF K=0 THEN 00145
00140 PRINT J;" TO THE POWER OF ";K
00145 NEXT J
00150 PRINT
00155 REM AROUND WE GO AGAIN
00160 GOTO 00055
00165 END
```

PRIME NUMBER

This program computes the first n primes from 1 to n. The limit of the number of primes found is 500. To change this, increase the DIM statement in line 40. Remember that the bigger the DIM assignment the more memory required.

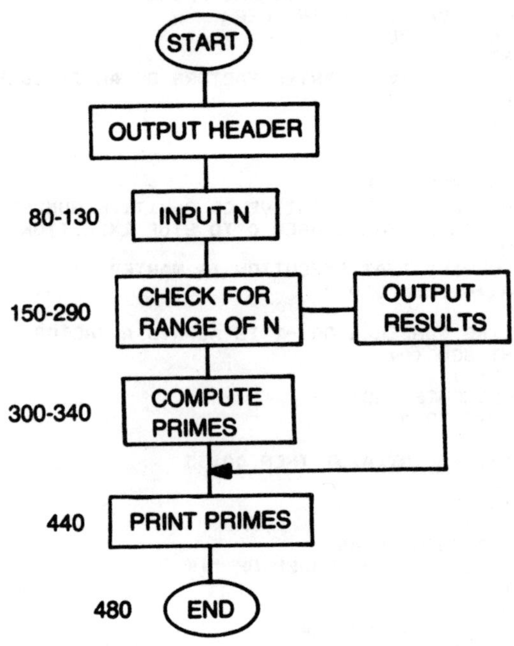

Prime Number

EXAMPLE

```
THIS PROGRAM COMPUTES ALL KNOWN PRIMES
FROM 1 TO N
N = ? 100
ALL PRIMES HAVE NOW BEEN LOCATED
THERE ARE  26  PRIMES UP TO AND INCLUDING  100

PRIME #          PRIME
 1                1
 2                2
 3                3
 4                5
 5                7
 6                11
 7                13
 8                17
 9                19
 10               23
 11               29
 12               31
 13               37
 14               41
 15               43
 16               47
 17               53
 18               59
 19               61
 20               67
 21               71
 22               73
 23               79
 24               83
 25               89
 26               97

WE ARE NOW FINISHED

SRU       0.228 UNTS.

RUN COMPLETE.
```

PROGRAM

```
00010 REM A PRIME NUMBER GENERATOR
00020 REM KT APRIL 1978
00030 REM ALLOW UP TO 500 PRIMES TO BE FOUND
00040 DIM P(500)
00050 PRINT
00060 PRINT"THIS PROGRAM COMPUTES ALL KNOWN PRIMES"
00070 PRINT"FROM 1 TO N"
00080 PRINT"N =";
00090 INPUT N
00100 IF N>1 THEN 00150
00110 REM YOU GOOFED-IT MESSAGE
00120 PRINT"OKAY WISE-GUY, ALL PRIMES ARE GREATER THAN ZERO"
00130 GOTO 00080
00140 REM CHECK WHERE WE ARE
00150 P(1)=1
00160 L=1
00170 IF N<2 THEN 00390
00180 P(2)=2
00190 L=2
00200 IF N<3 THEN 00390
00210 P(3)=3
00220 L=3
00230 IF N<5 THEN 00390
00240 P(4)=5
00250 L=4
00260 I=5
00270 I=I+2
00280 IF I>N THEN 00390
00290 J=3
00300 X=I/P(J)
00310 IF X=INT(X) THEN 00270
00320 IF X<P(J+1) THEN 00350
00330 J=J+1
00340 GOTO 00300
00350 L=L+1
00360 REM ASSIGN THE PRIMES
00370 P(L)=I
00380 GOTO 00270
00390 PRINT"ALL PRIMES HAVE NOW BEEN LOCATED"
00400 PRINT"THERE ARE ";L;" PRIMES UP TO AND INCLUDING ";N
00410 PRINT
00420 PRINT"PRIME #","PRIME"
00430 FOR I=1 TO L
00440 PRINT I,P(I)
00450 NEXT I
00460 PRINT
00470 PRINT"WE ARE NOW FINISHED"
00480 END
```

RESISTIVE PI AND T NETWORKS

This program computes the Pi and T resistor networks using as information the desired loss in dB and the input and output impedances (resistances).

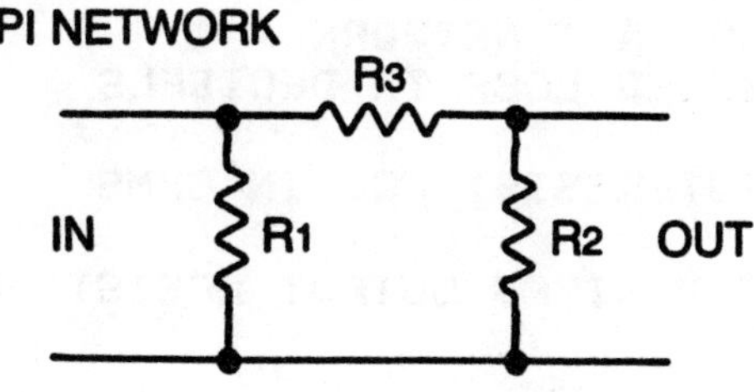

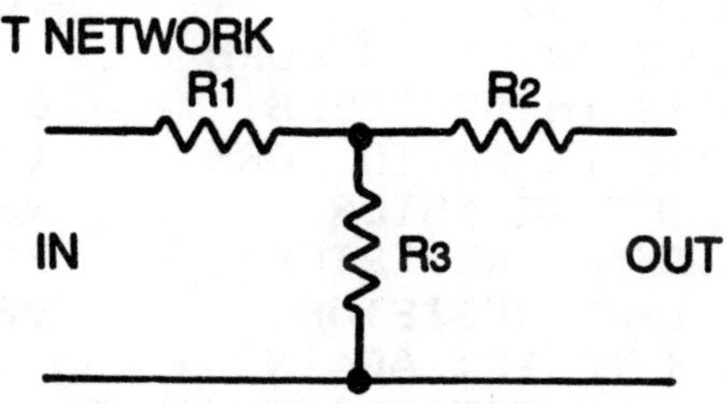

PI Network

EXAMPLE

```
ENTER 1 FOR A PI NETWORK
ENTER 0 FOR A T NETWORK ? 0
ENTER DESIRED LOSS IN DECIBELS
? 10
ENTER INPUT RESISTANCE IN OHMS
? 50
ENTER THE DESIRED OUTPUT RESISTANCE
? 50

T-ATTENUATOR RESULTS
INPUT RESISTANCE                       50
OUTPUT RESISTANCE                      50
DESIRED LOSS(DB)                       10
DESIRED LOSS IN RATIO FORM             10
MINIMUM LOSS IN DECIBELS               0
MINIMUM LOSS IN RATIO FORM             1
VALUE OF LEFT RESISTOR                 25.9747
VALUE OF CENTER RESISTOR               35.1364
VALUE OF RIGHT RESISTOR                25.9747
DO YOU WISH TO TRY AGAIN?
ENTER 1 TO TRY DIFFERENT VALUES 0 TO STOP
? 1
ENTER 1 FOR A PI NETWORK
ENTER 0 FOR A T NETWORK ? 1
ENTER DESIRED LOSS IN DECIBELS
? 10
ENTER INPUT RESISTANCE IN OHMS
? 50
ENTER THE DESIRED OUTPUT RESISTANCE
? 50

PI ATTENUATOR RESULTS
INPUT RESISTANCE                       50
OUTPUT RESISTANCE                      50
DESIRED LOSS(DB)                       10
DESIRED LOSS IN RATIO FORM             10
MINIMUM LOSS IN DECIBELS               0
MINIMUM LOSS IN RATIO FORM             1
VALUE OF LEFT RESISTOR                 96.2475
VALUE OF CENTER RESISTOR               71.1512
VALUE OF RIGHT RESISTOR                96.2475
DO YOU WISH TO TRY AGAIN?
ENTER 1 TO TRY DIFFERENT VALUES 0 TO STOP
? 0
```

```
PROGRAM   RESATT

ENTER 1 FOR A PI NETWORK
ENTER 0 FOR A T NETWORK ? 0
ENTER DESIRED LOSS IN DECIBELS
? 2
ENTER INPUT RESISTANCE IN OHMS
? 75
ENTER THE DESIRED OUTPUT RESISTANCE
? 100
OUTPUT RESISTANCE EXCEEDS INPUT
ENTER INPUT RESISTANCE IN OHMS
? -3
 THE VALUE JUST ENTERED IS INVALID
 RESISTANCES MUST BE POSITIVE
ENTER INPUT RESISTANCE IN OHMS
? 75
ENTER THE DESIRED OUTPUT RESISTANCE
? 50
 DESIRED LOSS < MIN LOSS OF  5.71948
CORRECT AND RE-ENTER VALUES
ENTER DESIRED LOSS IN DECIBELS
? 6
ENTER INPUT RESISTANCE IN OHMS
? 75
ENTER THE DESIRED OUTPUT RESISTANCE
? 50

T ATTENUATOR RESULTS
INPUT RESISTANCE                 75
OUTPUT RESISTANCE                50
DESIRED LOSS(DB)                 6
DESIRED LOSS IN RATIO FORM       3.98107
MINIMUM LOSS IN DECIBELS         5.71948
MINIMUM LOSS IN RATIO FORM       3.73205
VALUE OF LEFT RESISTOR           43.344
VALUE OF CENTER RESISTOR         81.9734
VALUE OF RIGHT RESISTOR          1.57153
DO YOU WISH TO TRY AGAIN?
ENTER 1 TO TRY DIFFERENT VALUES 0 TO STOP
? 9
DO YOU WISH TO TRY AGAIN?
ENTER 1 TO TRY DIFFERENT VALUES 0 TO STOP
? 1
```

```
ENTER 1 FOR A PI NETWORK
ENTER 0 FOR A T NETWORK ? 9
ENTER 1 FOR A PI NETWORK
ENTER 0 FOR A T NETWORK ? 1
ENTER DESIRED LOSS IN DECIBELS
? 6
ENTER INPUT RESISTANCE IN OHMS
? 75
ENTER THE DESIRED OUTPUT RESISTANCE
? 50

PI ATTENUATOR RESULTS
INPUT RESISTANCE                    75
OUTPUT RESISTANCE                   50
DESIRED LOSS(DB)                    6
DESIRED LOSS IN RATIO FORM          3.98107
MINIMUM LOSS IN DECIBELS            5.71948
MINIMUM LOSS IN RATIO FORM          3.73205
VALUE OF LEFT RESISTOR              2386.2
VALUE OF CENTER RESISTOR            45.7465
VALUE OF RIGHT RESISTOR             86.5171
DO YOU WISH TO TRY AGAIN?
ENTER 1 TO TRY DIFFERENT VALUES 0 TO STOP
? 0
```

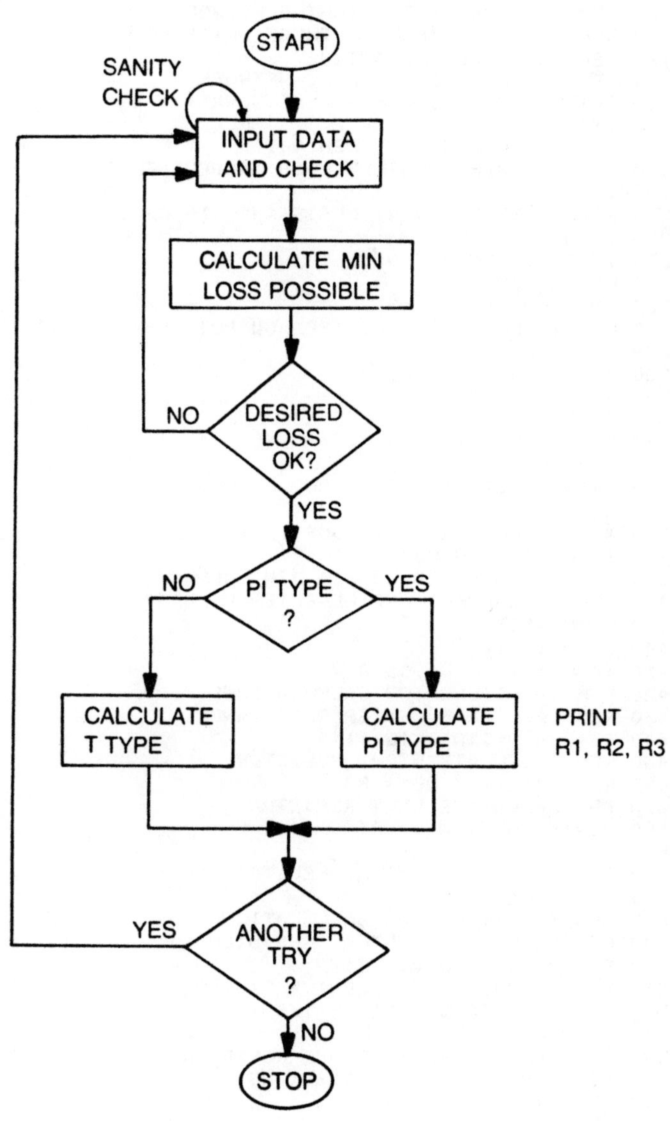

Resistive PI and T Networks

PROGRAM

```
00100 REM THIS PROGRAM CALCULATES THE VALUES REQUIRED
00110 REM FOR EITHER A PI OR T ATTENUATOR
00120 REM OR IMPEDANCE MATCHING NETWORK
00130 REM THE IMPEDANCE OF THESE UNITS
00140 REM IS PURELY RESISTIVE
00150 PRINT "ENTER 1 FOR A PI NETWORK"
00160 PRINT "ENTER 0 FOR A T NETWORK";
00170 INPUT O
00180 IF O<>1 AND O <>0 THEN 00150
00190 PRINT "ENTER DESIRED LOSS IN DECIBELS"
00200 INPUT L
00210 PRINT "ENTER INPUT RESISTANCE IN OHMS"
00220 INPUT I
00230 IF I>0 THEN 00260
00240 GOSUB 00780
00250 GOTO 00210
00260 PRINT "ENTER THE DESIRED OUTPUT RESISTANCE"
00270 INPUT O1
00280 IF O1> 0 THEN 00310
00290 GOSUB 00780
00300 GOTO 00260
00310 IF I < O1 THEN 00330
00320 GOTO 00350
00330 PRINT "OUTPUT RESISTANCE EXCEEDS INPUT"
00340 GOTO 00210
00350 M1=20*LOG(SQR(I/O1)+SQR(I/O1-1))/LOG(10)
00360 IF L>M1 THEN 00400
00370 PRINT " DESIRED LOSS < MIN LOSS OF ";M1
00380 PRINT "CORRECT AND RE-ENTER VALUES"
00390 GOTO 00190
00400 Q=10^(L/10)
00410 IF O = 1 THEN 00520
00420 REM T- ATTENUATOR CALCULATIONS
00430 REM CALCULATE CENTER RESISTANCE
00440 R3=SQR(Q*I*O1)/(Q-1)*2
00450 REM CALCULATE RIGHT RESISTOR
00460 R2=O1*(Q+1)/(Q-1)-R3
00470 REM CALCULATE LEFT RESISTOR
00480 R1=I*(Q+1)/(Q-1)-R3
00490 PRINT
00500 PRINT "T-ATTENUATOR RESULTS"
00510 GOTO 00630
00520 REM PI ATTENUATOR CALCULATIONS
00530 REM CALCULATE CENTRAL RESISTOR
00540 R3=SQR(I*O1/Q)*(Q-1)/2
00550 REM CALCULATE THE LEFT RESISTOR
00560 R1=(1/I)*(Q+1)/(Q-1)-(1/R3)
00570 R1=1/R1
00580 REM CALCULATE THE RIGHT RESISTOR
00590 R2=(1/O1)*(Q+1)/(Q-1)-(1/R3)
00600 R2=1/R2
00610 PRINT
00620 PRINT "PI ATTENUATOR RESULTS"
00630 PRINT "INPUT RESISTANCE",I
00640 PRINT "OUTPUT RESISTANCE",O1
00650 PRINT "DESIRED LOSS(DB)",L
00660 PRINT "DESIRED LOSS IN RATIO FORM",Q
00670 PRINT "MINIMUM LOSS IN DECIBELS",M1
00680 PRINT "MINIMUM LOSS IN RATIO FORM",10^(M1/10)
00690 PRINT "VALUE OF LEFT RESISTOR",R1
```

```
00700 PRINT 'VALUE OF CENTER RESISTOR',R3
00710 PRINT 'VALUE OF RIGHT RESISTOR',R2
00720 PRINT 'DO YOU WISH TO TRY AGAIN?'
00730 PRINT 'ENTER 1 TO TRY DIFFERENT VALUES 0 TO STOP'
00740 INPUT O
00750 IF O=1 THEN 00150
00760 IF O=0 THEN 00820
00770 GOTO 00720
00780 REM SUBROUTINE TO PRINT MESSAGE
00790 PRINT ' THE VALUE JUST ENTERED IS INVALID'
00800 PRINT ' RESISTANCES MUST BE POSITIVE'
00810 RETURN
00820 END
```

RESISTANCE IN PARALLEL AND SERIES

This program will compute either parallel or series resistance for up to 100 resistors.

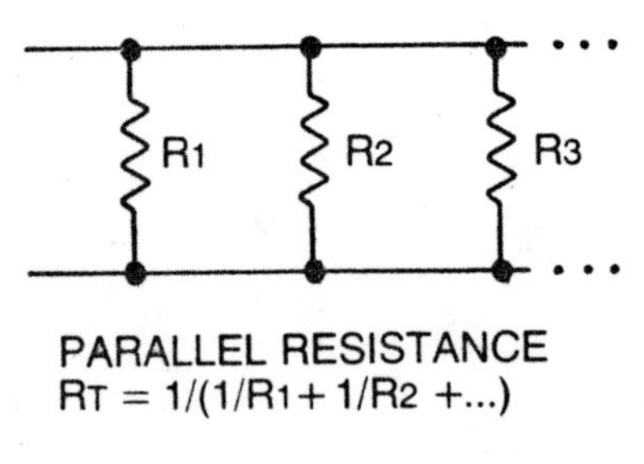

PARALLEL RESISTANCE
$R_T = 1/(1/R_1 + 1/R_2 + \ldots)$

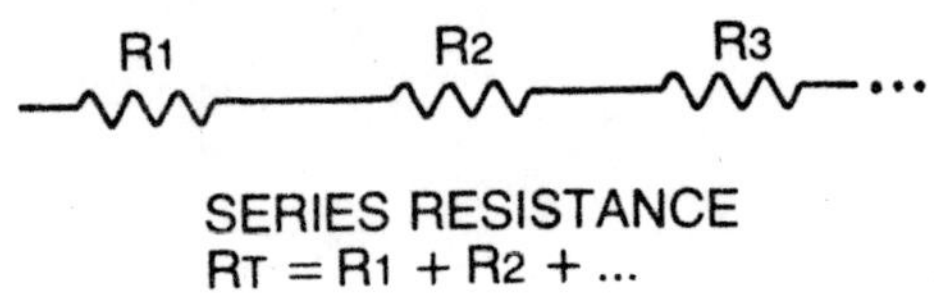

SERIES RESISTANCE
$R_T = R_1 + R_2 + \ldots$

```
RESISTANCE IN PARALLEL & SERIES

RUN

TYPE 1 FOR PARALLEL, 2 FOR SERIES

? 1

HOW MANY RESISTORS

? 2

RESISTOR 1 = 10

RESISTOR 2 = 10

TOTAL PARALLEL RESISTANCE = 5 OHMS
TYPE 1 FOR PARALLEL, 2 FOR SERIES

? 2
HOW MANY RESISTORS

? 3
RESISTOR 1 = 15

RESISTOR 2 = 10
RESISTOR 3 = 5

TOTAL SERIES RESISTANCE = 30 OHMS
RUN COMPLETE
```

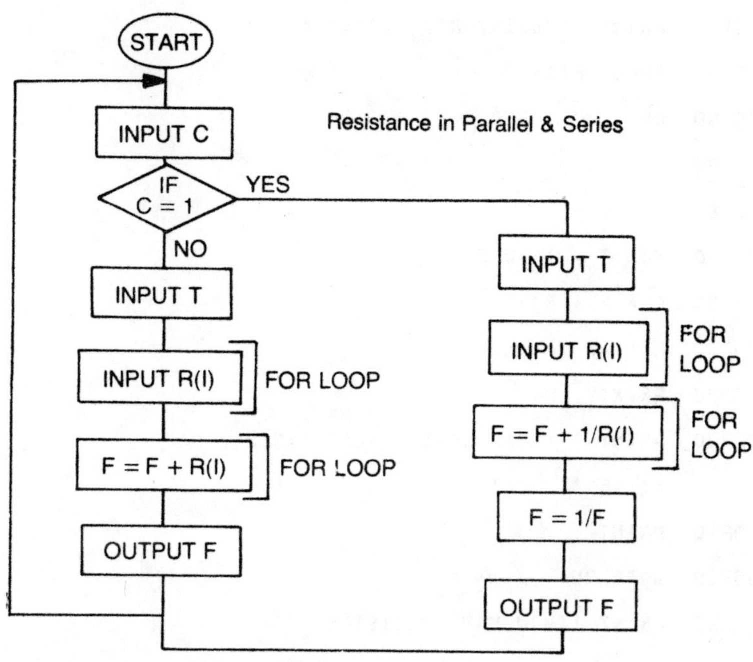

Resistance in Parallel & Series

PROGRAM

```
00010  REM THIS PROGRAM COMPUTES BOTH
00020  REM SERIES AND PARALLEL
       RESISTANCES
00030  REM KT 1978
00040  DIM R{100}
00050  REM START
00060  PRINT
00070  PRINT ''TYPE 1 FOR PARALLEL, 2
       FOR SERIES''
00080  INPUT C
00090  IF C = 1 THEN 260
00100  PRINT
00110  PRINT ''HOW MANY RESISTORS''
00120  INPUT T
00130  FOR I = 1 TO T
00140  PRINT ''RESISTOR'';I;''='';
00150  INPUT R{I}
00160  PRINT
00170  NEXT I
00180  F = 0
00190  FOR I = 1 TO T
00200  F = F + R{I}
00210  NEXT I
00220  PRINT
00230  PRINT ''TOTAL SERIES RESISTANCE
       ='';F;''OHMS''
00240  PRINT
00250  GOTO 70
00260  PRINT ''HOW MANY RESISTORS''
```

```
00270  INPUT T
00280  FOR I = 1 TO T
00290  PRINT ''RESISTOR '';I;''='';
00300  INPUT R{I}
00310  PRINT
00320  NEXT I
00330  F = 0
00340  FOR I = 1 TO T
00350  F = F + {1/R{I}}
00360  NEXT I
00370  F = 1/F
00380  PRINT
00390  PRINT ''TOTAL PARALLEL
       RESISTANCE ='';F; ''OHMS''
00400  PRINT
00410  GOTO 70
00420  END
```

RELIABILITY

This program computes the reliability of a system with components. Information required is the number of hours of operation of the system in question, the number of components comprising the system, and the wearout and failure factors.

```
EXAMPLE
*******RELIABILITY OF A SYSTEM*******

NUMBER OF HOURS OF OPERATION, 0 TO STOP
? 12

ENTER THE NUMBER OF COMPONENTS IN THE SYSTEM
? 3
COMPONENT # 1
AVERAGE TIME TO WEAROUT
? 1000
AVERAGE RATE OF FAILURE
? .09
COMPONENT # 2
AVERAGE TIME TO WEAROUT
? 234
AVERAGE RATE OF FAILURE
? .009
COMPONENT # 3
AVERAGE TIME TO WEAROUT
? 1567
AVERAGE RATE OF FAILURE
? .008
```

```
RELIABILITY OF SYSTEM IS  .257963

NUMBER OF HOURS OF OPERATION, 0 TO STOP
? 1000

ENTER THE NUMBER OF COMPONENTS IN THE SYSTEM
? 5
COMPONENT # 1
AVERAGE TIME TO WEAROUT
? 12
AVERAGE RATE OF FAILURE
? .5
COMPONENT # 2
AVERAGE TIME TO WEAROUT
? 1200
AVERAGE RATE OF FAILURE
? .09
COMPONENT # 3
AVERAGE TIME TO WEAROUT
? 120
AVERAGE RATE OF FAILURE
? .01
COMPONENT # 4
AVERAGE TIME TO WEAROUT
? 4
AVERAGE RATE OF FAILURE
? .8
COMPONENT # 5
AVERAGE TIME TO WEAROUT
? 345
AVERAGE RATE OF FAILURE
? .02

RELIABILITY OF SYSTEM IS  0

NUMBER OF HOURS OF OPERATION, 0 TO STOP
? 0
```

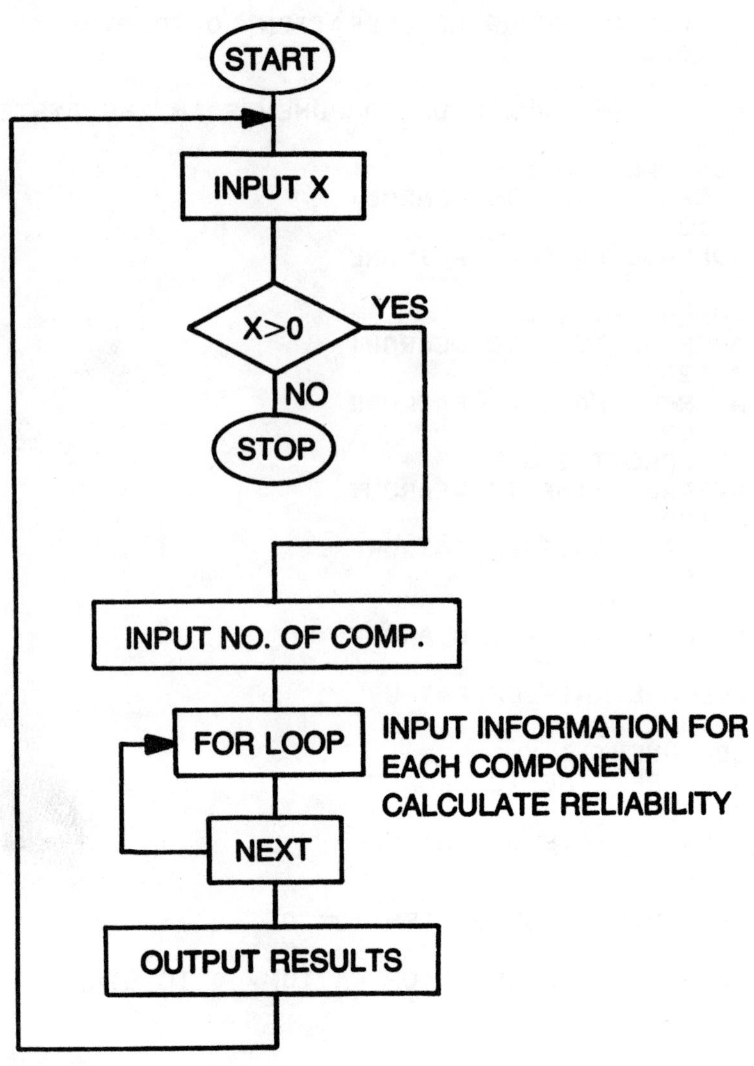

Reliability

PROGRAM

```
00005 REM THIS PROGRAM COMPUTES RELIABILITY OF A SYSTEM
00010 REM KT 12/3/78
00015 PRINT
00020 PRINT"*******RELIABILITY OF A SYSTEM*******"
00025 PRINT
00030 PRINT"NUMBER OF HOURS OF OPERATION, 0 TO STOP"
00035 INPUT X
00040 IF X>0 THEN 00050
00045 STOP
00050 PRINT
00055 PRINT"ENTER THE NUMBER OF COMPONENTS IN THE SYSTEM"
00060 INPUT Y
00065 Q=0
00070 FOR J=1 TO Y
00075 PRINT"COMPONENT #";J
00080 PRINT"AVERAGE TIME TO WEAROUT"
00085 INPUT T
00090 PRINT"AVERAGE RATE OF FAILURE"
00095 INPUT R
00100 Q=Q+1/T+R
00105 NEXT J
00110 PRINT
00115 Q=EXP(-Q*X)
00120 PRINT"RELIABILITY OF SYSTEM IS ";Q
00125 PRINT
00130 GOTO 00030
00135 END
```

APPENDIX

The brief programs included in this appendix are of great use to those working in electronics. They give quick solutions to those quantities that are repeatedly needed during the course of everyday calculations.

```
EXAMPLE

PROGRAM

FREQUENCY TO WAVELENGTH

10  REM FIND WAVELENGTH

20  PRINT ''ENTER FREQUENCY IN MHZ''

30  INPUT X

40  M = 300/X

50  PRINT ''WAVELENGTH IS '';M;''
    METERS''

60  END
```

WAVELENGTH TO FREQUENCY

```
10  REM FINDING FREQUENCY
20  PRINT ''ENTER WAVELENGTH IN METERS''
30  INPUT M
40  F = 300*M
50  PRINT ''FREQUENCY IS '';F;''MHZ''
60  END
```

HALF-WAVE ANTENNA LENGTH

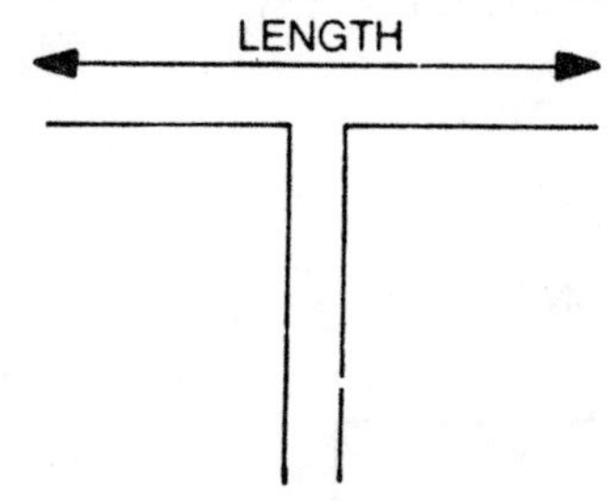

HALF-WAVE ANTENNA LENGTH

```
10  REM FIND ANTENNA LENGTH
20  PRINT ''ENTER FREQUENCY IN MHZ''
30  INPUT X
40  F = 468/X
60  PRINT ''LENGTH IS '';F;''FEET''
70  END
```

LC RESONANCE FREQUENCY

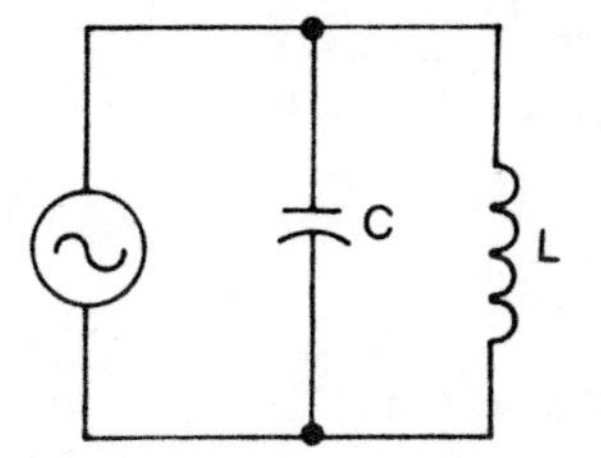

LC RESONANCE FREQUENCY

```
10  REM FREQUENCY OF RESONANCE
20  PRINT ''INPUT CAPACITANCE IN
    FARADS''
30  INPUT E
40  PRINT ''INPUT INDUCTANCE IN
    HENRYS''
50  INPUT H
60  F = 1/2*3.1415 X{SQR{E/H}}
70  PRINT ''RESONANT FREQUENCY = '';
    F;''HERTZ''
80  END
```

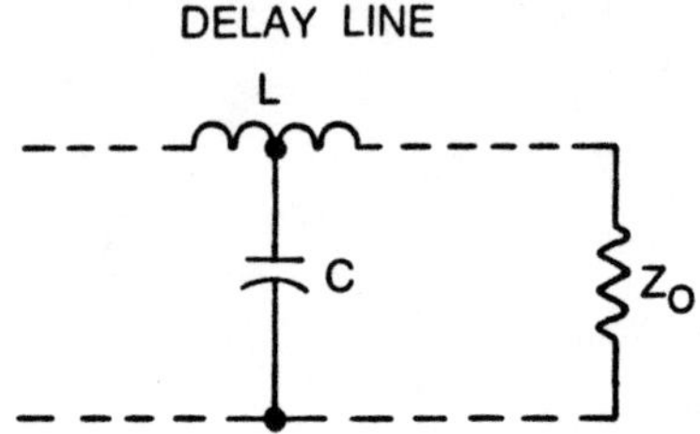

$f_o = 0.45/T$
$C = \tau/Z_o = M/\pi f_o Z_o$
$\tau = M/\pi f_o$
$L = MZ_o/\pi f_o$
T = RISE TIME IN SECONDS
f_o = CUTOFF FREQ IN HZ
τ = TIME DELAY PER SECOND

FIND T

```
10  REM DELAY LINE FIND T
20  PRINT ''ENTER FO IN HZ''
30  INPUT F
40  T = 0.45/F
50  PRINT ''TIME IN SECONDS = '';T
60  END
```

FIND F_0

```
10  REM DELAY LINE FIND F0
20  PRINT ''ENTER T IN SECONDS''
30  INPUT T
40  F = 0.45/T
50  PRINT ''CUT OFF FREQUENCY IN HZ
    = '';F
60  END
```

FIND L

```
10  REM DELAY LINE FIND INDUCTANCE
20  PRINT ''ENTER OUTPUT IMPEDANCE ZO''
30  INPUT Z
40  PRINT ''ENTER TIME DELAY IN
    SECONDS''
50  INPUT T
60  Q = T*Z
70  PRINT ''INDUCTANCE = '';Q
80  END
```

RISE TIME

```
10  REM RISE TIME
20  PRINT ''ENTER BANDWIDTH IN HZ''
30  INPUT B
40  R = 0.35/B
50  PRINT ''RISE TIME IN SECONDS =
    '';R
60  END
```

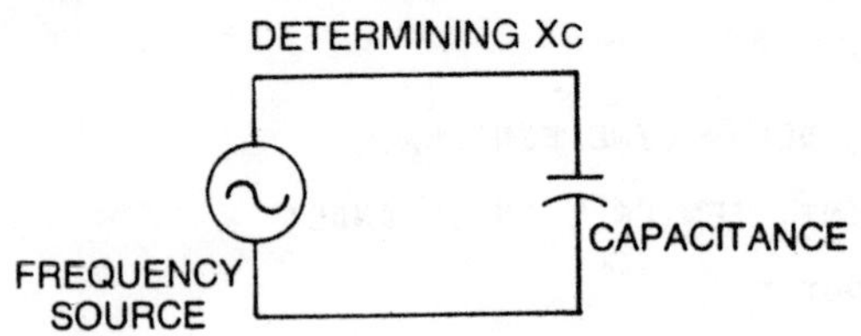

DETERMINING X_C

```
10  REM FIND XC
20  PRINT ''ENTER C IN FARADS''
30  INPUT C
40  PRINT ''ENTER F IN HZ''
50  INPUT F
60  X = 1/C*F*2*3.1415
70  PRINT ''REACTANCE = '';X;''OHMS''
80  END
```

POWER TO DB

```
10  REM DECIBEL CONVERTER POWER GAIN
20  PRINT ''ENTER GAIN {POWER}''
30  INPUT X
40  Z = 10*{LOG{X}/LOG{10}}
50  PRINT Z; ''DB''
60  END
```

VOLTAGE TO DB

```
10  REM DECIBEL CONVERTER VOLTAGE GAIN
20  PRINT ''ENTER GAIN {VOLTAGE}''
30  INPUT X
40  Z = 20*{LOG{X}/LOG{10}}
50  PRINT Z;''DB''
60  END
```

VOLTAGE GAIN IN DB

```
10  REM VOLTAGE GAIN IN DB
20  PRINT ''HIGHER VOLTAGE''
30  INPUT V2
40  PRINT ''LOWER VOLTAGE''
50  INPUT V1
60  0 = 20{LOG{V2/V1}/LOG{10}}
70  PRINT ''VOLTAGE GAIN = '';D;''DB''
80  END
```

POWER GAIN IN DB

```
10  REM POWER GAIN IN DB
20  PRINT ''HIGHER POWER''
30  INPUT P2
40  PRINT ''LOWER POWER''
50  INPUT P1
60  D = 10*{LOG{P2/P1}/LOG{10}}
70  PRINT ''POWER GAIN = '';D;''DB''
80  END
```

TRANSISTOR BETA

```
10  REM BETA
20  PRINT ''INPUT BASE CURRENT''
30  INPUT B
40  PRINT ''INPUT COLLECTOR CURRENT''
50  INPUT C
60  T = C/B
70  PRINT ''FORWARD CURRENT TRANSFER
    RATIO = '';T
80  END
```

TRANSISTOR BETA

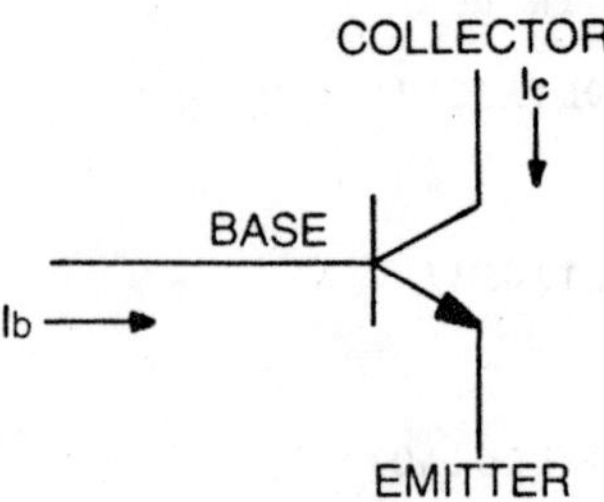

FORCE

```
10  REM FIND FORCE
20  PRINT ''ENTER MASS IN KG''
30  INPUT M
40  PRINT ''ENTER ACCELERATION IN
    M/SEC/SEC''
50  INPUT A
60  F = M*A
70  PRINT ''FORCE = '';F;''NEWTONS''
80  PRINT ''FORCE = '';F*1E05;''DYNES
    AS WELL''
90  END
```

Index